Decoding Antiquity

Volume One

# Challenging the Ancient Astronaut Myth

## John A Gillam

Independent Writer On Antiquity

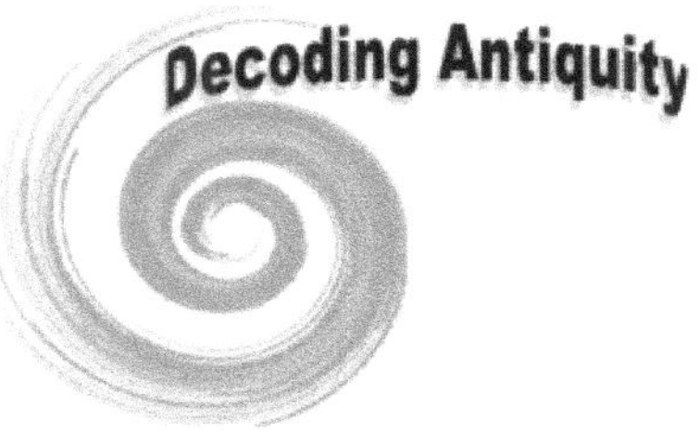

# Table of Contents

# PUBLICATION DETATILS



Cover illustration by Jeremy Zero (Unsplash™)

First edition August 2024

Published by Decoding Antiquity, Canberra.

A division of Creative Horizons Healthcare.

ABN 87 866 904 801.

www.decodingantiquity.weebly.com

# ACKNOWLEDGMENTS

I would like to express my gratitude to all those who supported and inspired me throughout the writing of this book. To my wife and friends, thank you for your encouragement. To the readers of this book, thank you for your interest in decoding our modern myth about ancient astronauts.

I would also like to extend my heartfelt appreciation to the numerous authors and researchers whose works I have referenced throughout this book. Your dedication to uncovering the truth and sharing your knowledge has been invaluable to my own research and writing processes. Without your tireless efforts and insightful contributions, this book would not have been possible.

To all the scholars, archaeologists, historians, and scientists whose work has shed light on the incredible achievements of our ancient ancestors, I am deeply grateful. Your commitment to rigorous research and evidence-based analysis has been a constant source of inspiration and guidance.

# PREFACE

The marvels of ancient civilizations and the extraordinary feats that they accomplished have long captivated me. From the towering pyramids of Ancient Egypt to the intricate stonework of Machu Picchu, the evidence of our ancestors' brilliance and skill is etched into the very fabric of our world. However, I have grown increasingly concerned about the proliferation of theories attributing these wonders to the intervention of ancient astronauts.

While I do not discount the possibility of extraterrestrial life or even the potential for alien visitation, I firmly believe that the achievements of our ancient forebears are a testament to their intelligence, creativity, and determination. The notion that these accomplishments required the guidance and technology of advanced alien beings is, in my view, a disservice to the memory of our ancestors and the legacy they left behind.

I write this book not to dismiss those who believe in ancient alien theories, but to offer an alternative perspective that celebrates the incredible abilities of our own species. I hope that readers will come to see our ancient ancestors in a new light — not as primitive beings in need of extraterrestrial intervention, but as brilliant innovators and problem-solvers who laid the foundations for the world we inhabit today.

Together, let us celebrate the extraordinary capabilities of our ancestors and the rich tapestry of human history that has brought us to where we are today.

John A. Gillam

# GLOSSARY

———

**A**boriginal: Relating to the Indigenous peoples of Australia, who have inhabited the continent for upwards of 60,000 years according to current research.

**Ancient astronaut theory**: The pseudoscientific belief that intelligent extraterrestrial beings visited Earth in antiquity and made contact with humans, influencing the development of cultures, technologies, and religions.

**Ancient mythology**: The collection of myths, stories, and legends created by ancient civilizations to explain the world around them, often involving gods, heroes, and supernatural beings.

**Anthropomorphic**: Attributed with human characteristics or behavior; in this context, it refers to the depiction of mythological beings or spirits in human-like form.

**Antikythera Mechanism**: An ancient Greek astronomical calculator, dated to around 150-100 BCE, which used complex gears and dials to predict the positions of celestial bodies and track the cycles of the ancient Olympic Games.

**Anunnaki**: The term 'Anunnaki' originates from ancient Mesopotamian mythology, particularly in Sumerian, Akkadian, Assyrian, and Babylonian texts. The Anunnaki were considered to be a group of deities associated with the ancient pantheon, believed to be offspring of the sky god Anu and the earth goddess Ki. They played various roles in myths, including the creation of humanity and the administration of the cosmos and the underworld.

**Apocryphal stories**: Narratives of doubtful authenticity or authorship that are not considered part of the canonical religious texts.

**Archaeology**: The study of human history and prehistory through the excavation and analysis of artifacts, physical remains, and other evidence.

**Baghdad Battery**: A set of three artifacts found in Khujut Rabu, near Baghdad, Iraq, in 1936, consisting of a clay jar, a copper cylinder, and an iron rod, which some believe could have been used for electroplating or generating electricity in ancient times.

**Baiame**: A creator god in the mythology of several Aboriginal groups in southeastern Australia, often misinterpreted by ancient astronaut theorists as an extraterrestrial being.

**Bradshaw rock paintings** (Gwion art): Enigmatic red ochre paintings in the Kimberley region of Western Australia depicting human figures, sometimes misinterpreted as extraterrestrial beings by fringe theorists.

**Collective Unconscious**: A concept proposed by Carl Jung, referring to a shared, inherited collection of knowledge, images, and archetypes that are universal among all humans and influence our behavior and thoughts.

**Constantinean Donation** (Donatio Constantini): A forged 8th-century document purporting to record Roman Emperor Constantine the Great's transfer of authority over Rome and the western part of the Roman Empire to Pope Sylvester I.

**Cosmology**: A set of beliefs and knowledge about the origin, structure, and evolution of the universe, both in scientific and cultural contexts.

**Cuneiform**: One of the earliest known systems of writing, originating in ancient Mesopotamia, consisting of wedge-shaped impressions made on clay tablets.

**Deus ex machina**: A plot device whereby a seemingly unsolvable problem in a story is abruptly resolved by an unexpected and unlikely occurrence, often interpreted in this context as referring to extraterrestrial intervention in human affairs.

**Dreamtime**: A term used to describe the Australian Aboriginal cosmology, mythology, and spiritual beliefs surrounding the creation of the world.

# CHALLENGING THE ANCIENT ASTRONAUT MYTH

**Erich von Däniken**: A Swiss author who popularized the 'ancient astronaut' theory in his 1968 book *Chariots of the Gods?* and subsequent works.

**Extraterrestrial Hypothesis**: The idea that some UFO sightings and encounters can be explained by the presence of intelligent life from other planets visiting Earth.

**Fringe theory**: An idea or viewpoint that significantly departs from mainstream or conventional thinking in a field of study.

**Kentril Tablets**: A set of stone slabs allegedly discovered in Morocco, purporting to contain Ancient Punic writing, but later exposed as modern forgeries.

**Nazca Lines**: A series of massive geoglyphs etched into the desert floor in the Nazca Desert, Peru, depicting various animals, humanoid figures, and geometric shapes, believed to have been created by the Nazca culture between 500 BCE and 500 CE.

**Nephilim**: The Nephilim have been described as being a race of giants and hybrids. Therefore they had a mixture of human and alien DNA. According to the *Book of Enoch* (and the *Bible*), the Nephilim were massive in physical size; they had great influence and access to hidden knowledge; and, they had unusual power and abilities.

**Olmecs**: An ancient Mesoamerican civilization that flourished in the present-day Mexican states of Veracruz and Tabasco.

**Piri Reis Map**: A 16th-century Ottoman naval map, created by admiral and cartographer Piri Reis, which depicts parts of Europe, North Africa, and the coast of Brazil with surprising accuracy for its time and from an 'aerial' perspective.

**Popol Vuh**: A sacred text of the K'iche' people, one of the Maya peoples, containing a collection of myths and histories describing the creation of the world and the legendary heroes.

**Pseudoscience**: A collection of beliefs or practices mistakenly regarded as being based on the scientific method.

**Radiometric dating**: A technique used to date materials based on the known decay rate of radioactive isotopes present in the material.

**Rock art**: Human-made markings on stone, including petroglyphs (carvings or engravings) and pictographs (paintings or drawings), often in a spiritual or symbolic context.

**Saqqara Bird**: A small wooden artifact discovered in the tomb of the ancient Egyptian official Pa-di-Imen in Saqqara, Egypt, in 1898, which resembles a bird or a glider and has led to speculation about the ancient Egyptians' knowledge of aviation.

**Sumerian cuneiform**: The written script of the ancient Sumerian civilization, consisting of logographic and syllabic elements inscribed on clay tablets.

**UFO** (Unidentified Flying Object): An object seen in the sky that cannot be immediately identified or explained, often associated with extraterrestrial spacecraft. The USA government introduced the term 'Unidentified Aerial Phenomena' (UAP) in 2019 as a term to replace UFO. The change in terminology reflects a shift in focus from the idea of extraterrestrial spacecraft to a more neutral, catch-all term for any unexplained aerial sightings, regardless of their origin or nature. This includes not only potential extraterrestrial vehicles but also foreign adversaries' advanced technology, natural atmospheric phenomena, or other unidentified objects.

**Vimana**: In ancient Hindu texts and mythology, a flying machine or vehicle described as being used by gods, demigods, and legendary human figures, often with capabilities beyond conventional human technology.

**Wandjina**: Cloud and rain spirits in the mythology of several Indigenous groups in northern Australia, depicted in rock art and sometimes misinterpreted as extraterrestrial beings.

# CHAPTER ONE

# The enduring allure of ancient astronauts: Decoding a modern myth

―――

*The ancient astronaut hypothesis is a modern myth that cleverly intertwines our fascination with the cosmos with our inherent need to ascribe meaning and purpose to the human experience. By attributing the achievements of ancient civilizations to extraterrestrial intervention, we not only diminish the ingenuity of our ancestors but also create a narrative that reflects contemporary anxieties and desires about technology and our place in the universe*

*Jason Colavito, The Cult of Alien Gods, 2005.*

Since the dawn of human civilization, we have demonstrated an innate curiosity about our cosmic origins. Where did we come from? What forces shaped our primordial development as a species? This fundamental drive to understand our place in the universe has manifested in rich creation mythologies across cultures worldwide [1]. While these ancient stories once provided profound metaphorical context, the modern era has seen a particularly gripping origin myth take hold -— the controversial idea that extraterrestrial beings visited our ancestors in prehistory and profoundly shaped human civilization [2].

This chapter explores the enduring allure of the ancient astronaut theory, tracing its origins from early mythologies to its modern incarnation as a worldwide subculture. We will examine how this myth has developed over millennia, its intersection with UFO culture, and the significant role media has played in propagating these ideas. By deconstructing the ancient astronaut myth, we aim to understand its appeal, analyze its flaws, and appreciate the genuine marvels of human achievement that it often obscures.

# JOHN GILLAM

## Defining the ancient astronaut myth

The ancient astronaut myth, in its most basic form, posits that extraterrestrial beings visited Earth in the distant past and played a significant role in the development of human civilization. Proponents of this theory argue that these alien visitors were responsible for:

1. Influencing or directly assisting in the construction of ancient monuments and structures
2. Imparting advanced knowledge and technology to early human societies
3. Genetically engineering or modifying early humans
4. Appearing in ancient artwork and religious texts as gods or otherworldly beings.

While variations of this theory exist, the core claim remains consistent: That human civilization as we know it owes its rapid advancement to extraterrestrial intervention.

The modern iteration of this theory can be traced to the late 1960s and the wildly popular book *Chariots of the Gods?* by Swiss author Erich von Däniken. Building on fringe speculation from decades prior, von Däniken controversially suggested that archaeological artifacts and ancient texts contained tangible evidence of advanced extraterrestrials making contact with early societies like the Sumerians, Egyptians, and Mayans [3].

Despite being criticized by mainstream historians and scientists for its pseudoscientific arguments, von Däniken's sensationalistic theories resonated with the public and opened a new genre of ancient astronaut speculative writing [4]. In the ensuing decades, numerous authors like Zecharia Sitchin, Robert Temple, and David Childress built upon von Däniken's work, each adding their unique interpretations of artifacts, texts, and myths as circumstantial evidence reinforcing core ancient alien narratives [5].

# CHALLENGING THE ANCIENT ASTRONAUT MYTH

## Historical origins and development

While the modern ancient astronaut theory gained prominence in the mid-20th century, its roots can be traced back to the mythologies and religious traditions of ancient cultures. Many creation myths feature gods or divine beings descending from the heavens to interact with humans, which some ancient astronaut theorists interpret as early accounts of extraterrestrial contact.

Recent research has shed light on potential astronomical events that may have influenced early mythologies. The Younger Dryas Impact Hypothesis (YDIH) proposes that a fragmented comet from the Taurid meteor stream struck the Earth around 12,800 years ago, triggering widespread destruction and the onset of a millennium-long cooling period known as the Younger Dryas. This catastrophic event could have left an indelible mark on the collective memory of early human populations, potentially being recorded in ancient mythologies [6].

Meteor swarm with fire serpent— AI generated compilation from Wiki.

The idea of fiery serpents or dragons in the sky, a common motif in many ancient cultures, might have originated from witnessing multiple comet fragments streaking across the sky. These celestial phenomena could have appeared as writhing, serpentine forms, which then became woven into mythic narratives. This primal mythology of celestial serpents may have set the stage for the later emergence of ancient alien narratives, as the notion of powerful beings descending from the heavens was already ingrained in human imagination.

Even religious texts have been subject to reinterpretation by ancient astronaut theorists. For instance, the Old Testament of the *Bible* mentions meteor swarms hitting Earth in Numbers 21:6-9. While this passage is primarily meant to convey a message about faith and divine power, some have interpreted it as an ancient attempt to explain and understand a catastrophic celestial event. The intense light, heat, and trails of debris left by the meteors as they entered Earth's atmosphere might have appeared to ancient observers as serpents made of fire streaking across the sky.

The modern ancient astronaut theory also has roots in the occult and esoteric traditions of the late 19th and early 20th centuries. Helena Blavatsky's Theosophy, which blended Eastern and Western mysticism, introduced concepts of advanced beings from other worlds influencing human evolution. These ideas, while not directly proposing extraterrestrial visitation, laid the groundwork for later speculation about otherworldly intervention in human affairs [7].

## The UFO connection

The ancient astronaut theory gained significant momentum in the mid-20th century, coinciding with the rise of UFO culture. The phenomenon of unidentified flying objects, which gained widespread public attention following World War II, provided a modern context for interpreting ancient accounts of celestial visitors.

The connection between ancient astronaut theories and UFO sightings can be traced back to the early days of the flying saucer era. Reports of strange aerial phenomena during World War I and II fueled speculation about advanced technology potentially of extraterrestrial origin. As public interest in UFOs grew in the post-war years, some researchers began to draw parallels between modern sightings and ancient accounts of gods or celestial beings [8].

Newspaper report concerning the Roswell Army Air Field (RAAF), 1947 — Wikipedia

One of the earliest influential works to explicitly connect ancient myths with extraterrestrial visitation was *The Flying Saucers Have Landed* (1953) by Desmond Leslie and George Adamski. Leslie's portion of the book argued that references to flying crafts in ancient texts were evidence of prehistoric alien contact. This blend of ancient mythology and modern UFO culture set the stage for the more comprehensive ancient astronaut theories that would follow [9].

The 1960s saw a surge in UFO sightings and public interest in extraterrestrial life, creating a receptive audience for ancient astronaut ideas. The Space Race between the United States and the Soviet Union captured the public's imagination and fueled speculation about the possibility of extraterrestrial life [10]. This cultural climate, combined with the counterculture movement's growing interest in alternative spirituality and worldviews, provided fertile ground for the ancient astronaut theory to take root [11].

Erich von Däniken's *Chariots of the Gods?* capitalized on this cultural zeitgeist, presenting ancient alien visitation as a plausible explanation for various archaeological mysteries. The book's success spawned numerous imitators and helped solidify the connection between ancient history and modern UFO phenomena in the public imagination.

# CHALLENGING THE ANCIENT ASTRONAUT MYTH

## Media's role in propagating the myth

The influence of popular media in perpetuating the ancient astronaut myth cannot be overstated. Books, films, television shows, and more recently, the internet, have played a crucial role in spreading and legitimizing these ideas in the public consciousness.

Following the success of *Chariots of the Gods?*, a flood of books on the subject hit the market. Zecharia Sitchin's *The 12th Planet* (1976) became particularly influential, hypothesizing about mythological Anunnaki beings from the planet Nibiru and blending pseudoscientific claims with reinterpretations of ancient Sumerian texts [12].

Hollywood also embraced ancient astronaut themes, with films like *2001: A Space Odyssey* (1968) and *Stargate* (1994) popularizing the idea of alien influence on human civilization. These fictional portrayals, while not claiming to be factual, nonetheless helped to normalize the concept in popular culture [13].

Television has been perhaps the most potent medium for spreading ancient astronaut ideas. Documentary-style shows like *In Search Of...* (1977-1982) and later, *Ancient Aliens* on the History Channel, have presented these theories to millions of viewers. *Ancient Aliens*, which premiered in 2009, has been particularly influential in bringing ancient astronaut ideas into the mainstream.

Prometheus Entertainment

These television programs often present ancient astronaut theorists as credible academic sources, repackaging dubious pseudo-archaeological ideas with dramatic music and editing to present them as plausible 'alternative viewpoints' on human origins [14]. This approach generates renewed fascination with ancient astronauts, despite a lack of substantiating empirical evidence [15].

By presenting pseudoscientific ideas alongside legitimate archaeological and historical evidence, these programs create a false equivalence that can mislead audiences into believing that the ancient astronaut theory is a credible alternative to established scientific knowledge [16]. The use of persuasive rhetorical devices, such as appeals to authority and the bandwagon effect, have further enhanced the perceived credibility of ancient astronaut claims [17].

The rise of the internet has significantly amplified both ancient astronaut ideology and the countercultures formed around seeking evidence to validate these beliefs. Online communities have facilitated self-perpetuating feedback loops and 'citizen archaeology' aiming to uncover physical proof of prehistoric extraterrestrial contact, often using schismatic analysis techniques that lack scientific rigor [18]. Confirmation bias has allowed ambiguous or mundane artifacts like the Nazca Lines to be radically reinterpreted as potential 'landing strips' for alien visitors, perpetuating a cycle of misinformation [19].

## Psychological and cultural factors

The enduring popularity of the ancient astronaut theory can be attributed to various psychological and cultural factors that tap into fundamental human desires and cognitive biases.

- <u>Search for meaning</u>

  The ancient astronaut theory reflects broader cultural anxieties and desires, such as the fear of human insignificance in the face of a vast universe and the hope for a higher purpose or meaning to our existence [20]. In an increasingly secular and scientifically-oriented world, the idea of ancient astronauts provides a way for people to reconcile their desire for spiritual meaning with their fascination with science and technology [21].

- <u>Simplification of complex ideas</u>

The theory offers a simple, grand explanation for the complexities of human civilization [22]. It provides an easy-to-understand narrative that explains various archaeological and historical mysteries without requiring in-depth knowledge of multiple scientific disciplines.

- <u>Human exceptionalism</u>

The idea that our species' development was guided by a higher intelligence appeals to the notion of human exceptionalism [23]. It suggests that humans are special and chosen, rather than the product of natural evolutionary processes.

- <u>Distrust of mainstream institutions</u>

For some, embracing alternative theories like ancient astronauts represents a rejection of established academic and scientific institutions. This can be particularly appealing in times of social unrest or when trust in traditional authorities is low [24].

- <u>Pattern recognition and pareidolia</u>

Humans are naturally inclined to see patterns and make connections, even where none exist. This tendency, combined with pareidolia (the perception of familiar patterns where none are present), can lead people to see 'evidence' of ancient astronauts in various artifacts and structures [25]

- <u>Confirmation Bias</u>

Once someone becomes invested in the ancient astronaut theory, they may selectively seek out information that confirms their beliefs while dismissing contradictory evidence [26].

## Scientific and archaeological perspectives

From a scientific and archaeological standpoint, the ancient astronaut theory faces numerous challenges and criticisms:

- <u>Lack of physical evidence</u>

Despite decades of searching, no concrete physical evidence of ancient extraterrestrial visitation has been found. The artifacts and structures cited by ancient astronaut theorists can be explained through known human capabilities and technologies of the time [27].

- <u>Misinterpretation of ancient texts</u>

Many of the ancient texts used to support the theory are taken out of context or interpreted literally when they were likely meant to be metaphorical or allegorical [28].

- <u>Underestimation of human capabilities</u>

The theory often fails to recognize the remarkable achievements and capabilities of ancient civilizations, as evidenced by their awe-inspiring megalithic structures, precise astronomical alignments, and sophisticated engineering feats [29].

- <u>Lack of genetic evidence</u>

If extraterrestrials had intervened in human evolution or interbred with humans, as some ancient astronaut theorists suggest, we would expect to find evidence of this in the human genome. No such evidence has been found [30].

- <u>Reliance on pseudoscience</u>

Many of the methods used to support ancient astronaut claims, such as dowsing or psychic archaeology, are not considered valid scientific techniques [31].

- <u>Ignoring cultural context</u>

The theory often ignores the cultural and historical context of ancient artifacts and structures, imposing modern interpretations on objects that had very different meanings to their creators [32].

Recent advancements in fields like archaeology, anthropology, and genetics have provided compelling evidence for the remarkable capabilities of ancient human societies. For example, the discovery of sophisticated water management systems at the ancient city of Petra in Jordan, as well as the existence of complex astronomical knowledge among the Maya and other ancient cultures, demonstrates the ingenuity and intellectual sophistication of our ancestors [33].

Mayan astronomical observatory, Chichén Itzá, Mexico. Built circa 906 CE. – Mexican Government

## Conclusion

The ancient astronaut theory, while captivating to many, ultimately relies on misinterpretation of evidence, selective reasoning, and an underestimation of human capabilities. Its persistence in popular culture speaks to deep-seated human desires for meaning and connection to something greater than ourselves.

However, the real story of human achievement and ingenuity is far more compelling. By recognizing the genuine accomplishments of our predecessors, we can cultivate a deeper understanding of our shared human potential and the extraordinary feats we are capable of when knowledge is accumulated, shared, and built upon over centuries [34].

Critically examining the ancient astronaut theory provides valuable insights into the psychology behind belief in pseudoscientific ideas and the spread of misinformation. In our modern, interconnected world, developing critical thinking skills and scientific literacy is crucial for navigating the complex landscape of information and distinguishing fact from fiction [35].

As we continue to explore the mysteries of our past and push the boundaries of scientific discovery, we must remain grounded in evidence-based reasoning while maintaining a sense of wonder at the true marvels of human achievement throughout history. By doing so, we honor the ingenuity of our ancestors and pave the way for future discoveries that will continue to illuminate the fascinating story of human civilization [36].

<u>References</u>

[1] Wright, R. (2009). *The evolution of God*. Little, Brown and Company.

[2] Colavito, J. (2005). *The cult of alien gods: H.P. Lovecraft and extraterrestrial pop culture*. Prometheus Books.

[3] von Däniken, E. (1968). *Chariots of the Gods? Unsolved mysteries of the past*. Putnam.

[4] Feder, K. L. (2017). *Frauds, myths, and mysteries: Science and pseudoscience in archaeology* (9th ed.). Oxford University Press.

[5] Story, R. D. (1976). *The space-gods revealed: A close look at the theories of Erich von Däniken.* Harper & Row.

[6] Kennett, J. P., et al. (2015). Bayesian chronological analyses consistent with synchronous age of 12,835–12,735 Cal B.P. for Younger Dryas boundary on four continents. *Proceedings of the National Academy of Sciences, 112*(32), E4344-E4353. https://doi.org/10.1073/pnas.1507146112

[7] Hanegraaff, W. J. (1996). *New Age religion and Western culture: Esotericism in the mirror of secular thought.* Brill Publishing.

[8] Saler, B., Ziegler, C. A., & Moore, C. B. (1997). *UFO crash at Roswell: The genesis of a modern myth.* Smithsonian Institution Press.

[9] Leslie, D., & Adamski, G. (1953). *The flying saucers have landed.* British Book Centre.

[10] McCurdy, H. E. (2011). *Space and the American imagination.* Johns Hopkins University Press.

[11] Partridge, C. (Ed.). (2003). *UFO religions.* Routledge.

[12] Sitchin, Z. (1976). *The 12th planet.* Stein and Day.

[13] Kubrick, S. (Director). (1968). *2001: A space odyssey* [Film]. Metro-Goldwyn-Mayer.

[14] Fritze, R. H. (2009). *Invented knowledge: False history, fake science and pseudo-religions.* Reaktion Books.

[15] Ward, C., & Voas, D. (2011). The emergence of conspirituality. *Journal of Contemporary Religion, 26*(1), 103-121. https://doi.org/10.1080/13537903.2011.539846

[16] Barkun, M. (2013). *A culture of conspiracy: Apocalyptic visions in contemporary America* (Vol. 15). University of California Press.

[17] Uscinski, J. E., & Parent, J. M. (2014). *American conspiracy theories*. Oxford University Press.

[18] Lewandowsky, S., Ecker, U. K., & Cook, J. (2017). Beyond misinformation: Understanding and coping with the 'post-truth' era. *Journal of Applied Research in Memory and Cognition*, 6(4), 353-369. https://doi.org/10.1016/j.jarmac.2017.07.008

[19] Hines, T. (2003). *Pseudoscience and the paranormal*. Prometheus Books.

[20] Shermer, M. (2011). *The believing brain: From ghosts and gods to politics and conspiracies — How we construct beliefs and reinforce them as truths*. Henry Holt and Company.

[21] Partridge, C. (Ed.). (2003). *UFO religions*. Routledge.

[22] Stenger, V. J. (1990). *Physics and psychics: The search for a world beyond the senses*. Prometheus Books.

[23] Sagan, C. (1996). *The demon-haunted world: Science as a candle in the dark*. Random House.

[24] van Prooijen, J. W., & Douglas, K. M. (2017). Conspiracy theories as part of history: The role of societal crisis situations. *Memory Studies*, 10(3), 323-333. https://doi.org/10.1177/1750698017701615

[25] Shermer, M. (2002). *Why people believe weird things: Pseudoscience, superstition, and other confusions of our time* (Rev. and expanded ed.). Henry Holt & Company.

[26] Nickell, J. (2009). Return to Roswell. *Skeptical Inquirer*, 33(1), 10-12.

[27] Fagan, G. G. (Ed.). (2006). *Archaeological fantasies: How pseudoarcheology misrepresents the past and misleads the public*. Routledge.

[28] Smith, J. C. (2010). *Pseudoscience and extraordinary claims of the paranormal: A critical thinker's toolkit*. Wiley-Blackwell.

[29] Nielsen, R., Akey, J. M., Jakobsson, M., Pritchard, J. K., Tishkoff, S., & Willerslev, E. (2017). Tracing the peopling of the world through genomics. *Nature, 541*(7637), 302-310. https://doi.org/10.1038/nature21347

[30] Jordan, P. (2016). Astrobiology and the search for extraterrestrial life in the age of social media. *International Journal of Astrobiology, 15*(4), 271-277. https://doi.org/10.1017/S1473550416000136

[31] Pigliucci, M., & Boudry, M. (Eds.). (2013). *Philosophy of pseudoscience: Reconsidering the demarcation problem.* University of Chicago Press.

[32] Harrison, A. A. (1997). *After contact: The human response to extraterrestrial life.* Plenum Press.

[33] YouTube. (2024). *Secrets of the Nabataeans: Unraveling Ancient Mysteries* [Video]. https://www.youtube.com/watch?v=JKE3K3TrhWk

[34] Clancy, S. A. (2005). *Abducted: How people come to believe they were kidnapped by aliens.* Harvard University Press.

[35] Douglas, K. M., Sutton, R. M., & Cichocka, A. (2017). The psychology of conspiracy theories. *Current Directions in Psychological Science, 26*(6), 538-542. https://doi.org/10.1177/0963721417718261

[36] Feder, K. L. (2020). *Frauds, myths, and mysteries: Science and pseudoscience in archaeology* (10th ed.). Oxford University Press.

# CHAPTER TWO

# Human ingenuity in ancient megastructures

*Monuments like the Egyptian pyramids or Teotihuacán are so monumental, so precise, that many people assume they could not have been constructed by ancient societies with the technological limitations we tend to ascribe to them. This is a very modern, very Western form of arrogance.*

*Dr Michael Smith, archeologist, quoted in the article 'Past Salvaged: Pyramids as Protest Art' by Adam Langer in the New York Times,*

*13 November 2002.*

The monumental ruins and awe-inspiring structures left behind by ancient cultures have long captured the imagination of people worldwide. From the Egyptian pyramids to the megalithic temples of Malta and the colossal statues of Easter Island, these architectural wonders stand as testaments to the ingenuity, skill, and determination of our ancestors. While some fringe theorists have proposed that these structures could not have been built without the intervention of advanced extraterrestrial beings, a closer examination of the evidence reveals that human creativity and perseverance can indeed account for these incredible feats.

In-depth study of the construction methods employed by the ancient Egyptians reveals a remarkable level of sophistication and innovation. In reality, these ingenious builders knew how to take advantage of their environment and develop advanced techniques to meet the colossal challenges posed by the construction of the pyramids.

One of the most fascinating aspects of pyramid construction lies in the complex logistics put in place to transport the enormous stone blocks from the quarries to the construction sites. Contrary to previous hypotheses that assumed exclusively land-based transport, recent discoveries have shed light on the Egyptians' clever use of waterways.

Indeed, the geography of ancient Egypt offered a considerable natural advantage: the Nile and its tributaries. The builders were able to exploit this river network to facilitate the transport of heavy materials over long distances, thus significantly reducing the effort and time required to deliver the stone blocks.

Some of the most famous examples of ancient megalithic construction are the iconic structures of the pyramids of Saqqara and Giza, built around 2600 BCE. Recent research has illuminated the sophisticated techniques and tools employed by the ancient Egyptians to construct these marvels.

Saqqara, located about 30 kilometers south of modern-day Cairo, served as the main necropolis for the ancient Egyptian capital of Memphis. This vast burial ground spans over seven kilometers and was in use for more than 3,000 years, from the First Dynasty (circa 3100 BCE) to the Ptolemaic period (332-330 BCE). Saqqara is home to Egypt's oldest known pyramid, the Step Pyramid of Djoser, built around 2630 BCE. This revolutionary monument marked the transition from earlier mastaba tombs to the iconic pyramid shape, setting the stage for the grand pyramids that would follow.

The Giza Plateau, situated on the outskirts of Cairo, is perhaps the most famous archaeological site in Egypt, if not the world. It is home to the Great Pyramid of Khufu, the only surviving wonder of the ancient world, along with the pyramids of Khafre and Menkaure. Built during the Fourth Dynasty of the Old Kingdom period (circa 2686-2181 BCE), these pyramids represent the pinnacle of ancient Egyptian pyramid construction. The Giza complex also includes the enigmatic Great Sphinx, numerous smaller pyramids, and several cemeteries.

Both Saqqara and Giza were integral parts of the ancient Egyptians' elaborate belief system concerning the afterlife. These necropolises were not merely burial grounds but were considered gateways to the realm of the gods. The pyramids served as eternal homes for the pharaohs, designed to protect their bodies and possessions for the afterlife. The surrounding temples and structures were used for funerary rituals and the perpetual worship of the deceased kings.

Recent archaeological and geological studies have revealed that the ancient landscape of these areas was quite different from what we see today. The Nile River, the lifeblood of ancient Egyptian civilization, played a crucial role in the construction of these monumental structures. Evidence suggests that a now-dry branch of the Nile, known as the Ahramat Branch, once flowed much closer to the pyramid sites than the river's current course. At the time, this waterway was about half a kilometer wide and at least 25 meters deep. A study by an international team of scientists suggests that this branch of the Nile River was used for the transportation of heavy stone blocks by boat [1]. The discovery of an ancient papyrus in Egypt, known as the *Diary of Merer*, provides further evidence of the use of waterways to transport limestone blocks to the construction sites [2].

This proximity of the Nile and its branches to the construction sites was a key factor in the feasibility of building such massive structures. The following map illustrates the relative positions of the Saqqara and Giza areas, showing the ancient course of the Nile Branch and the associated waterways that were likely used for transporting building materials:

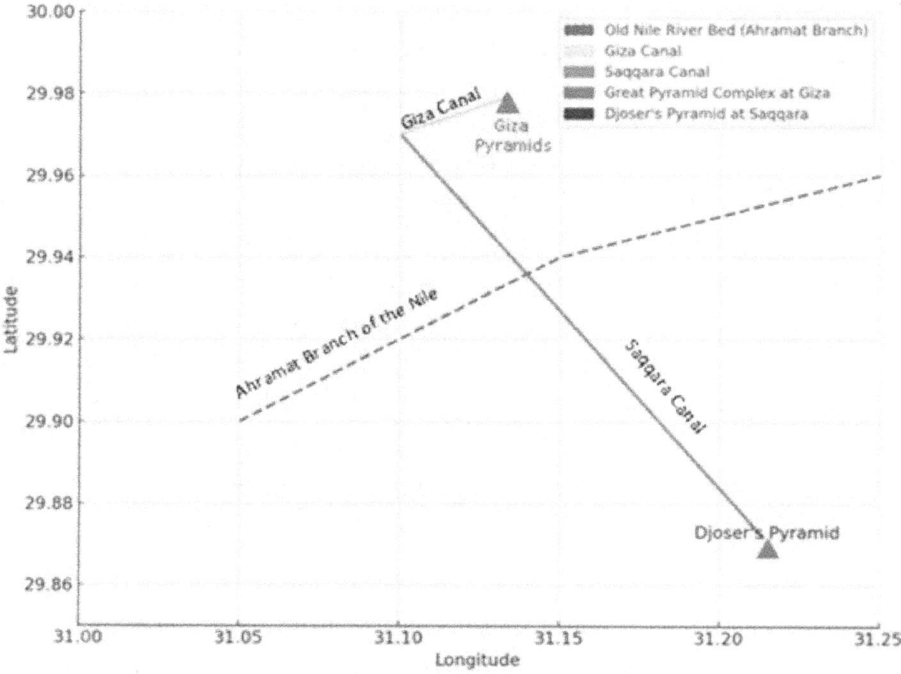


This reconstruction of the ancient landscape provides valuable insights into how the Egyptians might have transported the enormous stone blocks to construct the pyramids.

The alignment of the Giza pyramids with the cardinal directions has been a source of wonder and mystery. However, this feat can be explained by the Egyptians' advanced understanding of astronomy and surveying techniques. By observing the stars and using simple tools like plumb bobs and sighting instruments, the ancient builders were able to achieve remarkable accuracy in their construction [3]. The Ancient Egyptians' used a tool called a Merkhet to align the pyramids with the stars. They were correct to within less than half a degree. [4].

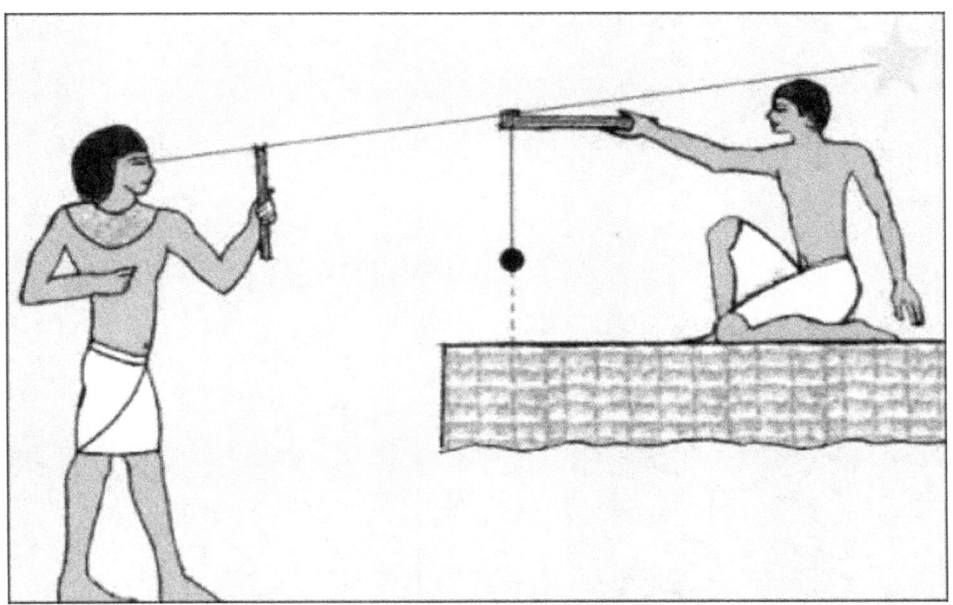

Ancient Egyptians used the Merkhet to align the pyramids with the stars.—Madison College Astronomy.

It is not only the alignment of the Great Pyramid complex with the cardinal points that has attracted ancient alien theorists, it is the spacing between the three main pyramids: Khufu (aka Cheops), Khafre, and Menkaure. The idea that the distance between these pyramids reflects the separation that we see in the three stars of Orion's Belt gained popularity with Robert Bauval's 1995 book, *The Orion Mystery* [5]. However, there is no physical evidence or mention in Egyptian texts to suggest that this was the builders' original intention. Astronomical calculations for the period around 2600 BCE show the pyramids' positions don't perfectly match the separation of the stars in Orion's Belt at that specific time.

Great Pyramid complex when first built.—[Digital reconstruction]—Anonymous.

When it comes to lifting the granite blocks into place, some new research suggests that the Ancient Egyptians used a hydraulic lift. This research is based on the building of the Pyramid of Djoser, also known as the Step Pyramid, which was a proto-pyramid built as the final resting place for Pharoah Djoser (2670-2650 BCE) of Egypt's Third Dynasty during the Old Kingdom period. For comparison, the Peruvian pyramids at Caral-Supe are contemporary, being built around 2600 BCE. However, the ziggurats of Mesopotamia predate these pyramids by about 400 years.

Pyramid of Djoser, Saqqare.

Pyramid at Caral-Supe, Peru

Ziggurat illustration, Mesopotamia

# CHALLENGING THE ANCIENT ASTRONAUT MYTH

Recent research on Djoser's Pyramid that comes from a French team of archaeologists suggests that the ancient Egyptians may have used hydraulic force to construct that pyramid [6]. This groundbreaking study proposes that a hydraulic lift system was employed to raise the massive stone blocks used in the pyramid's construction. Evidence supporting this claim includes:

- <u>Water management system</u>: The researchers found evidence of a complex water management system near the pyramid, including a possible check dam and an ephemeral lake.
- <u>Pyramid architecture</u>: The internal structure of the pyramid is consistent with a hydraulic elevation mechanism.
- <u>Egyptian hydraulic expertise</u>: The ancient Egyptians were known for their advanced knowledge of hydraulics, as demonstrated by their irrigation canals and barge systems.

If proven, this discovery of the use of hydraulic force to build the pyramids would revolutionize our understanding of ancient Egyptian engineering and construction techniques. However, this research deals only with the vertical lift of stones and does not detail how the stones were moved horizontally within the pyramid construction site.

The Great Pyramid of Khufu was built about 70 years after Djoser's Pyramid. That pyramid shows the advancement from the step design of Djoser's to the smooth-sided design exemplified by Khufu's pyramid. This progression illustrates the rapid advancement in Egyptian engineering and architectural techniques during the Old Kingdom period.

Another example of impressive ancient stonework can be found at the site of Puma Punku in Bolivia. The precisely cut and intricately fitted stone blocks at this site have led some theorists to propose that only advanced technology could have produced such work. However, a closer examination of the evidence reveals that the Tiwanaku culture, which built Puma Punku, had developed sophisticated stone-cutting techniques using tools made from hard metals like copper and bronze [7]. Experimental archaeology has also demonstrated that the precise fittings could have been achieved through the use of simple tools and techniques like grinding, sanding, and polishing [8].

Recent studies have also provided insights into the techniques used by the Tiwanaku to transport and position the massive stone blocks at Puma Punku. The use of ramps, levers, and rollers, similar to those employed by the ancient Egyptians, has been suggested as a possible method [9]. Additionally, the discovery of sandstone blocks with precisely drilled holes at the site indicates the use of a technique known as 'lofting', which involves the use of wooden templates and cords to ensure the accurate positioning of the stones [10].

The megalithic temples of Malta, such as the famous Ġgantija complex, are another testament to the capabilities of ancient builders. These structures, dating to approximately 3600 BCE, were constructed using massive limestone blocks weighing up to 50 tons [11]. While the transportation and erection of these blocks may seem impossible without modern machinery, evidence suggests that the ancient Maltese used a combination of levers, rollers, and ramps to move and position the stones [12]. The use of these simple but effective techniques, combined with careful planning and organization, allowed for the construction of these monumental structures. This innovative use of water transport was just one of many ingenious techniques employed by ancient builders.

Recent studies have also shed light on the tools and techniques used by the ancient Maltese to shape and decorate the limestone blocks used in the construction of the temples. The discovery of stone tools, including flint and obsidian blades, as well as stone hammers and chisels, provides evidence of the sophisticated stone working capabilities of the ancient Maltese [13]. Additionally, the intricate carvings and spiral designs found on many of the temple walls and floors have been studied using 3D scanning technology, revealing the incredible skill and precision of the ancient artisans [14].

Model of the Ġgantija temples.—National Museum of Archaeology, Malta.

Göbekli Tepe, a Neolithic site in southeastern Turkey, has also attracted attention for its complex megalithic structures and intricate carvings. Constructed around 9000 BCE, this site predates the invention of pottery, metallurgy, and even agriculture [15]. Some have argued that the construction of such an elaborate site by hunter-gatherers is evidence of external influence or advanced technology. However, recent research has shown that the people who built Göbekli Tepe had already developed a complex social structure and a deep understanding of their environment, which allowed them to pool their resources and labor to create this remarkable site [16].

Excavations at Göbekli Tepe have revealed a wealth of information about the tools and techniques used by the ancient builders. The discovery of stone tools, including flint and obsidian blades, as well as ground stone tools like axes and adzes, provides evidence of the sophisticated stone working capabilities of the Neolithic people [17]. Additionally, the use of rope and wooden rollers and levers has been suggested as a possible method for transporting and erecting the massive T-shaped pillars found at the site [18].

The moai statues of Easter Island have also been the subject of much speculation and mystery. These massive stone figures, some standing over 30 feet tall and weighing up to 80 tons, were carved from volcanic tuff and transported miles from the quarry to their final locations [19]. While some have suggested that the statues were moved using levitation or other supernatural means, archaeological evidence points to the use of wooden sleds, rollers, and ropes to transport the statues [20]. The oral traditions of the Rapa Nui people also describe the use of these techniques, passed down through generations [21].

Moai, Easter Island —Pixabay: LuisValiente

Recent studies have also provided insights into the tools and techniques used by the Rapa Nui to carve and shape the moai statues. The discovery of stone tools, including basalt chisels and obsidian blades, as well as the remains of wooden rollers and levers, provides evidence of the sophisticated stone working and engineering capabilities of the ancient Rapa Nui [22]. Additionally, experimental archaeology has demonstrated that the statues could have been transported using teams of people pulling on ropes attached to wooden sleds [23].

These examples demonstrate that the ancient builders of megalithic structures possessed a deep understanding of their environment, materials, and the principles of physics and engineering. Through careful observation, experimentation, and the passing down of knowledge through generations, these cultures were able to develop sophisticated techniques and tools to construct monumental works that continue to inspire and amaze us today.

It is essential to recognize that the construction of these megalithic structures was not the work of a single generation, but rather the result of centuries of accumulated knowledge, skills, and labor. The builders of these ancient wonders were not passive recipients of external knowledge, but active participants in a process of continuous learning, adaptation, and innovation. The development of new tools and techniques, such as the use of metal tools and the refinement of stone working methods, allowed for increasingly complex and ambitious construction projects over time [24].

Furthermore, the motivations behind the construction of these monumental works were deeply rooted in the cultural, spiritual, and social beliefs of the ancient societies that built them. The pyramids of Egypt, for example, were not merely impressive feats of engineering, but also powerful symbols of the divine status of the pharaohs and the belief in the afterlife [25]. The megalithic temples of Malta were likely centers of ritual and spiritual practice, reflecting the complex religious beliefs of the ancient Maltese [26]. Similarly, the moai statues of Easter Island were believed to embody the spirits of ancestral chiefs and provide protection and fertility to the island's inhabitants [27].

The construction of these megalithic structures also served important social and political functions within ancient societies. The ability to mobilize and organize large numbers of people for such monumental building projects was a demonstration of the power and authority of the ruling elites [28]. The construction process itself likely served as a means of social cohesion, bringing together people from different communities and social groups to work towards a common goal [29].

In conclusion, the evidence overwhelmingly supports the idea that human ingenuity, skill, and determination were the driving forces behind the construction of ancient megalithic structures. While there may still be some unanswered questions and mysteries surrounding these incredible feats of engineering, it is essential to approach these questions with a critical and evidence-based mindset, rather than resorting to speculation about advanced extraterrestrial intervention.

By acknowledging the capabilities and achievements of our ancestors, we can gain a deeper appreciation for the rich tapestry of human history and the incredible potential of the human spirit. The ancient builders of these monumental structures serve as an inspiration for us today, reminding us that with dedication, perseverance, and the sharing of knowledge, we too can achieve great things.

The study of ancient megalithic structures also has important implications for our understanding of the development of human civilization. The construction of these monumental works required not only advanced technical skills and knowledge but also complex social and political organization. The ability of ancient societies to mobilize and coordinate large numbers of people for such ambitious building projects demonstrates the emergence of hierarchical social structures and the development of centralized authority [30].

Furthermore, the spread of megalithic building traditions across different cultures and regions suggests the existence of long-distance trade networks and cultural exchanges in the ancient world. The similarities in building techniques and designs found in megalithic structures from Europe to Asia and beyond indicate that knowledge and ideas were being shared and adapted across vast distances [31].

The legacy of ancient megalithic structures extends far beyond their impressive physical remains. These monumental works have captured the imagination of people for centuries and continue to inspire awe and wonder in modern times. The study of these structures has also contributed to the development of new technologies and methods in fields such as archaeology, engineering, and materials science [32].

In recent years, advances in digital technologies have allowed for new insights into the construction and design of ancient megalithic structures. The use of 3D scanning and modeling techniques has enabled researchers to create detailed virtual reconstructions of these monuments, revealing previously unknown details and providing new perspectives on their architecture and symbolism [33]. These digital tools have also facilitated the sharing of knowledge and collaboration among researchers across different disciplines and regions.

The preservation and protection of ancient megalithic structures is an ongoing challenge that requires international cooperation and support. Many of these sites are threatened by factors such as climate change, urban development, and tourism pressures [34]. The development of sustainable tourism practices and the involvement of local communities in the management and interpretation of these sites are critical for their long-term preservation [35].

In addition to their cultural and historical significance, ancient megalithic structures also have important lessons to teach us about sustainability and resilience. The ability of ancient societies to construct such monumental works using locally available materials and renewable energy sources, such as human and animal labor, demonstrates the potential for sustainable building practices [36]. The longevity and durability of these structures, many of which have survived for thousands of years, also speaks to the importance of building for the long term and considering the impact of our actions on future generations.

In summary, the evidence overwhelmingly supports human ingenuity as the driving force behind ancient megalithic structures. While mysteries remain, a critical, evidence-based approach reveals the remarkable achievements of our ancestors. These structures demonstrate not only technical prowess but also complex social organization and cultural beliefs. They continue to inspire us today, offering valuable lessons about sustainability, social cohesion, and long-term thinking. By approaching these monuments with scientific rigor and respect, we can better appreciate the extraordinary capabilities of the human spirit throughout history.

References

[1] Lehner, M., & Hawass, Z. (2017). *Giza and the pyramids: The definitive history*. University of Chicago Press.

[2] Tallet, P. (2017). The harbor of Khufu on the Red Sea coast at Wadi al-Jarf, Egypt. *Near Eastern Archaeology, 80*(1), 4-9.

[3] Dash, G. (2011). Solar alignments of Giza. *Ancient Egypt Research Associates. Aeragram, 12*(2), 1-7.

[4] Belmonte, J. A. (2001). On the orientation of Old Kingdom Egyptian pyramids. *Journal for the History of Astronomy, 32*(1), S1-S20.

[5] Bauval, R., & Gilbert, A. (1995). *The Orion mystery: Unlocking the secrets of the pyramids*. Crown.

[6] Landreau, X. (2024). On the possible use of hydraulic force to assist with building the Step Pyramid of Saqqara. *Plus One*.

[7] Protzen, J. P., & Nair, S. E. (2002). Pumapunku: A Tiwanaku complex of monumental proportions. *Expedition, 44*(2), 25-28.

[8] Protzen, J. P. (1986). Inca stonemasonry. *Scientific American, 254*(2), 94-105.

[9] Vranich, A. (2010). The construction and reconstruction of ritual space at Tiwanaku, Bolivia (AD 500-1000). *Journal of Field Archaeology, 35*(2), 121-136.

[10] Protzen, J. P., & Nair, S. E. (2013). Who taught the Inca stonemasons their skills? A comparison of Tiwanaku and Inca cut-stone masonry. *Journal of the Society of Architectural Historians, 72*(1), 1-20.

[11] Trump, D. H. (2002). *Malta: Prehistory and temples*. Midsea Books.

[12] Torpiano, A. (2004). The construction of the prehistoric temples of Malta. In D. Cilia (Ed.), *Malta before history* (pp. 347-365). Miranda Publishers.

[13] Malone, C., Stoddart, S., Bonanno, A., & Trump, D. (Eds.). (2009). *Mortuary customs in prehistoric Malta: Excavations at the Brochtorff Circle at Xaghra (1987-1994)*. McDonald Institute for Archaeological Research.

[14] YouTube. (2023). *Megalithic Malta: The best preserved temples* [Video]. https://www.youtube.com/watch?v=UQmk8fQVt6Y

[15] Schmidt, K. (2010). Göbekli Tepe — The Stone Age sanctuaries. New results of ongoing excavations with a special focus on sculptures and high reliefs. *Documenta Praehistorica, 37*, 239-256.

[16] Dietrich, O., Heun, M., Notroff, J., Schmidt, K., & Zarnkow, M. (2012). The role of cult and feasting in the emergence of Neolithic communities. New

evidence from Göbekli Tepe, south-eastern Turkey. *Antiquity*, *86*(333), 674-695.

[17] Moorey, P. (1999). *Ancient Mesopotamian materials and industries: The archaeological evidence*. Eisenbrauns Imprint - Penn State University Press.

[18] Notroff, J., Dietrich, O., & Schmidt, K. (2016). Building monuments, creating communities: Early monumental architecture at Pre-Pottery Neolithic Göbekli Tepe. In J. Osborne (Ed.), *Approaching monumentality in archaeology* (pp. 83-105). SUNY Press.

[19] Van Tilburg, J. A. (1994). *Easter Island: Archaeology, ecology, and culture*. Smithsonian Institution Press.

[20] Hunt, T. L., & Lipo, C. P. (2011). *The statues that walked: Unraveling the mystery of Easter Island*. Free Press.

[21] Routledge, K. (1919). *The mystery of Easter Island*. Adventures Unlimited Press.

[22] Lipo, C. P., & Hunt, T. L. (2009). Revisiting Rapa Nui (Easter Island) 'Ecocide'. *Pacific Science*, *63*(4), 601-616.

[23] Lipo, C. P., Hunt, T. L., & Haoa, S. R. (2013). The 'walking' megalithic statues (moai) of Easter Island. *Journal of Archaeological Science*, *40*(6), 2859-2866.

[24] Renfrew, C., & Bahn, P. (2016). *Archaeology: Theories, methods and practice* (7th ed.). Thames & Hudson.

[25] Lehner, M. (1997). *The complete pyramids: Solving the ancient mysteries*. Thames & Hudson.

[26] Renfrew, C. (2004). Foreword. In D. Cilia (Ed.), *Malta before history* (pp. 13-15). Miranda Publishers.

[27] Van Tilburg, J. A. (2004). *Hoa Hakananai'a*. British Museum Press.

[28] Trigger, B. G. (1990). Monumental architecture: A thermodynamic explanation of symbolic behaviour. *World Archaeology, 22*(2), 119-132.

[29] Kolb, M. J. (2014). Monumentality and the rise of religious authority in precontact Hawai'i. *Current Anthropology, 55*(6), 695-714.

[30] Flannery, K. V., & Marcus, J. (2012). *The creation of inequality: How our prehistoric ancestors set the stage for monarchy, slavery, and empire.* Harvard University Press.

[31] Renfrew, C. (2001). Commodification and institution in group-oriented and individualizing societies. In W. G. Runciman (Ed.), *The origin of human social institutions* (pp. 93-117). Oxford University Press.

[32] Kintigh, K. W., et al. (2014). Grand challenges for archaeology. *American Antiquity, 79*(1), 5-24.

[33] Liritzis, I., & Castro, B. (2013). Delphi and cosmovision: Apollo's absence at the land of the hyperboreans and the time for consulting the oracle. *Journal of Astronomical History and Heritage, 16*(2), 184-206.

[34] Markham, A., Osipova, E., Lafrenz Samuels, K., & Caldas, A. (2016). *World heritage and tourism in a changing climate.* United Nations Environment Programme; United Nations Educational, Scientific and Cultural Organization.

[35] Auclair, E., & Fairclough, G. (Eds.). (2015). *Theory and practice in heritage and sustainability: Between past and future.* Routledge.

[36] Hashim, Z., Abdullah, S. A., & Nor, S. M. (2017, October). Stakeholders analysis on criteria for protected areas management categories in Peninsular Malaysia. In *IOP Conference Series: Earth and Environmental Science, 19*(1), 012014). IOP Publishing. DOI:10.1088/1755-1315/91/1/012014[1]

---

1. http://dx.doi.org/10.1088/1755-1315/91/1/012014

# CHAPTER THREE

# Archaeological anomalies and the ancient astronaut debate

*Human history is a saga of forgotten events, a narrative constructed upon shifting sands, our present understanding of which is but a fragile scaffolding that may collapse under the weight of new discoveries.*

*Graham Hancock, 1995*

*Fingerprints of the Gods: The Evidence of Earth's Lost Civilization*

The allure of mysterious artifacts and archaeological findings that challenge conventional historical narratives has long captivated the human imagination. These anomalies, often difficult to explain within the accepted framework of human technological development, have given rise to various theories, including the controversial ancient astronaut hypothesis. This chapter explores some of the most intriguing archaeological anomalies and their role in the ongoing debate surrounding the possibility of extraterrestrial intervention in human history.

One of the most prominent examples of alleged advanced technology in ancient times comes from the rich mythological tradition of India – the concept of vimanas. In various Sanskrit epics, *Puranas*, and Vedic literature, vimanas are described as flying machines or vehicles used by gods, demigods, and legendary human figures [1]. The most well-known references to vimanas can be found in the *Ramayana* and *Mahabharata*, two cornerstone texts of Hindu literature and culture.

In the *Ramayana*, a vimana is portrayed as a double-decked, circular aircraft with portholes and a dome, flown by the demon king Ravana [2]. The *Mahabharata* also mentions vimanas of various shapes and sizes, with some described as flying chariots with wheels, while others are said to be capable of changing shape during flight [3]. These vivid descriptions have led some to speculate that the ancient Indians possessed advanced aeronautical knowledge far ahead of their time.

Vimana Flying Machine — Wikidot

However, it is crucial to approach these mythological accounts with a critical eye. Most historians, archaeologists, and scholars of Hindu mythology interpret the vimana stories as part of a rich religious and literary tradition, often employing symbolism, allegory, and imaginative storytelling [4]. The fantastical descriptions of vimanas are generally understood as expressions of divine power, spiritual journeys, or the imaginative exploration of the concept of flight, rather than literal descriptions of advanced technological aircraft [5].

While some proponents of the ancient astronaut theory have suggested that vimanas were actual spacecraft piloted by extraterrestrial beings who visited Earth in antiquity, this idea lacks credible evidence and is not supported by mainstream scholars [6]. There is no reliable historical or archaeological evidence to suggest that such technologically advanced flying machines existed in ancient India.

Moving beyond the realm of mythology, there are numerous archaeological artifacts that have puzzled researchers and fueled speculation about ancient advanced technologies. One such example is the Antikythera mechanism, a complex geared device discovered in a shipwreck off the coast of the Greek island of Antikythera in 1901. Dating back to around 150-100 BCE, this intricate bronze mechanism consists of at least 30 interlocking gears and has been described as an ancient analog computer [7].

The Antikythera mechanism is believed to have been used for astronomical calculations to predict the positions of celestial bodies, and tracking the cycles of the ancient Olympic Games [8]. Its sophistication and precision have astounded scholars, as it demonstrates a level of technological achievement previously thought impossible for the ancient Greeks.

However, most experts agree that the Antikythera mechanism, while remarkably advanced for its time, is a testament to the ingenuity and scientific knowledge of the ancient Greeks [9]. The device's complexity can be attributed to the cumulative astronomical and mathematical knowledge developed by Greek scholars such as Hipparchus and Archimedes, rather than external intervention [10].

Reconstructed Antikythera Machine

*Original machine*
National Archaeological Museum

Another perplexing archaeological discovery is the Baghdad Battery, a set of three artifacts found in Khujut Rabu, near Baghdad, Iraq, in 1936. These objects, dating back to the Parthian period (200 BCE – 200 CE), consist of a clay jar, a copper cylinder, and an iron rod [11]. Some researchers have suggested that the Baghdad Battery could have been used for electroplating or even generating electricity, implying that the ancient Mesopotamians had a rudimentary understanding of electrical principles [12].

However, the theory that the Baghdad Battery was used for electrical purposes remains highly controversial and lacks conclusive evidence. Many scholars believe that the artifacts were likely used for storage or as ritual objects, rather than as an electrical device [13]. The absence of any written records or other archaeological evidence supporting the existence of electrical technology in ancient Mesopotamia further weakens the argument for the Baghdad Battery as proof of advanced ancient knowledge.

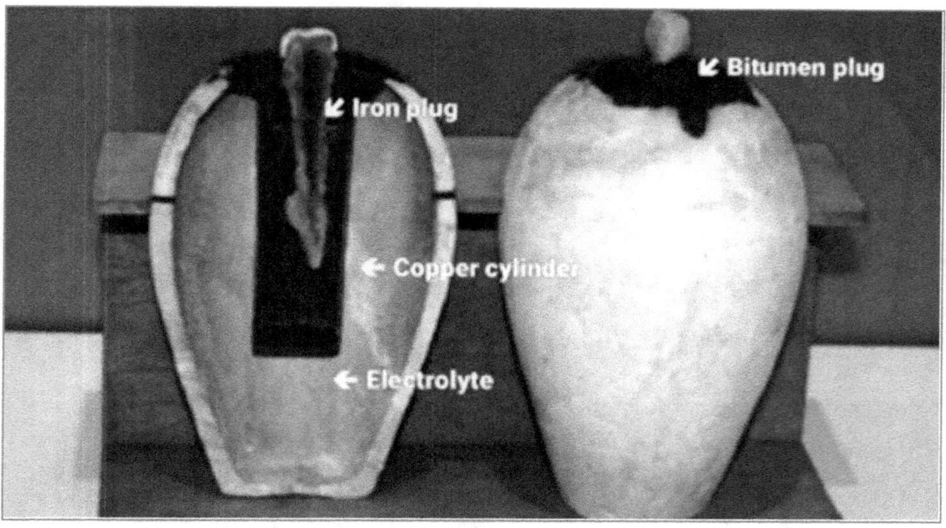


Baghdad Battery— Baghdad Museum

Modern archaeological techniques have significantly enhanced our understanding of these enigmatic artifacts. For instance, advanced dating methods such as thermoluminescence and radiocarbon dating have helped establish more precise chronologies for objects like the Baghdad Battery. Non-invasive imaging techniques, including X-ray computed tomography and multispectral imaging, have allowed researchers to examine the internal structures of artifacts like the Antikythera mechanism without risking damage.

Furthermore, materials science approaches, such as X-ray fluorescence spectroscopy, have provided insights into the composition and manufacturing techniques of these objects. These scientific methods, combined with contextual archaeological evidence, offer a more comprehensive and objective basis for interpreting these artifacts, often challenging sensationalist claims about their supposed advanced or otherworldly origins.

The Nazca Lines in Peru, a series of massive geoglyphs etched into the desert floor, have also been a source of fascination and mystery. These enormous drawings, some spanning hundreds of meters, depict various animals, humanoid figures, and geometric shapes, and can only be fully appreciated from the air [14]. The precision and scale of the Nazca Lines have led some ancient astronaut theorists to propose that they were created with the aid of extraterrestrial technology or as landing strips for alien spacecraft.

However, archaeological research has shown that the Nazca Lines were most likely created by the Nazca culture between 500 BCE and 500 CE, using simple tools and surveying techniques [15]. The geoglyphs are believed to have served ceremonial and religious purposes, possibly related to water and fertility rituals [16]. The idea that the Nazca Lines required alien intervention stems from a misunderstanding of the capabilities and motivations of the ancient Nazca people.

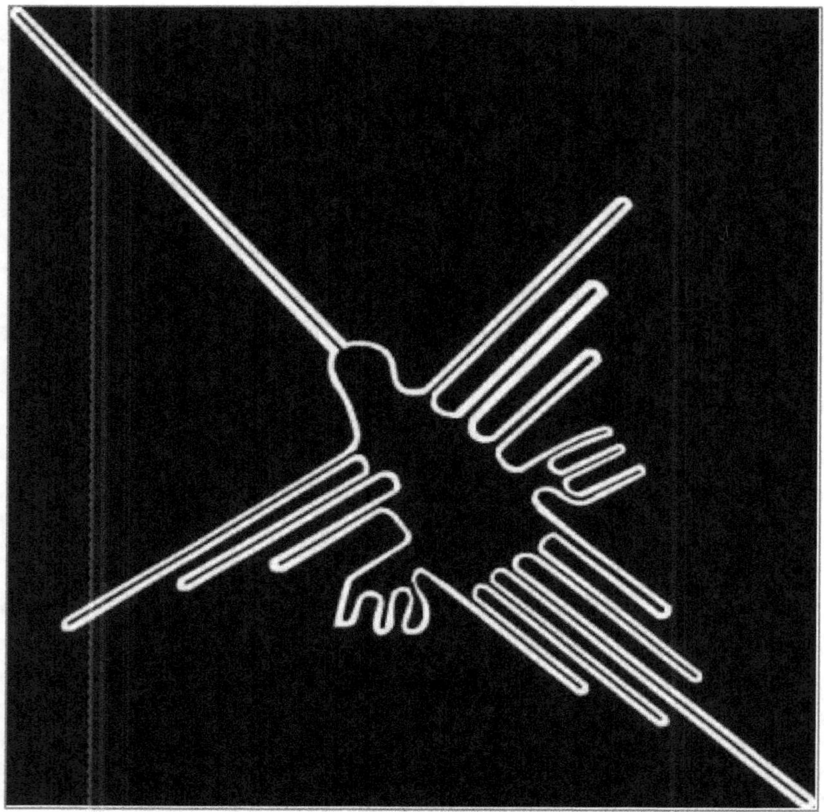

Nazca lines, Hummingbird example, Peru—Wikimedia

The Piri Reis map, a 16th-century Ottoman nautical chart, has also been a subject of controversy and speculation. The map, rediscovered in 1929, depicts parts of Europe, North Africa, and the coast of Brazil with surprising accuracy for its time [17]. Some fringe theorists have claimed that the map shows evidence of advanced geographical knowledge, including the coastline of Antarctica before its discovery, suggesting that the map's creators had access to aerial or satellite imagery.

However, mainstream scholars have debunked these claims, pointing out that the Piri Reis map is a compilation of various earlier maps and navigational charts, and its apparent accuracy is the result of skilled cartography rather than advanced technology [18]. The map's depiction of South America is consistent with the knowledge available to 16th-century explorers, and the alleged representation of Antarctica is more likely a distorted portrayal of the South American coastline [19].

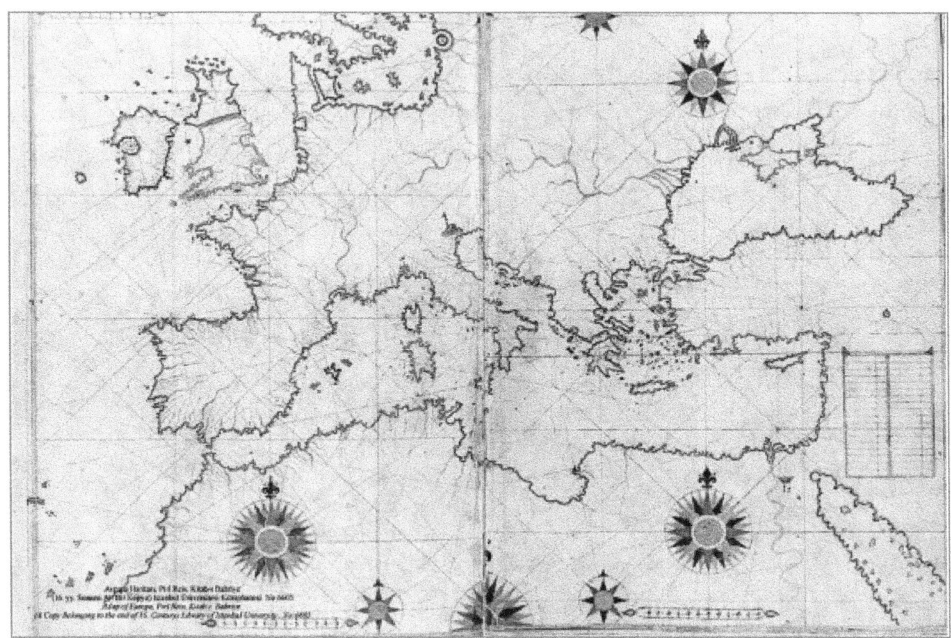

Piri Reis map — Wikipedia

Modern cartographic techniques have played a crucial role in interpreting and understanding historical maps like the Piri Reis chart. Geographic Information Systems (GIS) and digital mapping technologies have allowed researchers to overlay the Piri Reis map with modern, accurate maps, revealing both its strengths and inaccuracies. This process has helped scholars identify the sources Piri Reis likely used and understand the mapmaking techniques of the time. Additionally, advanced image analysis tools have enabled the examination of finer details and faded elements of the map, providing new insights into its creation and purpose. These modern approaches have largely debunked fringe theories about the map's supposed depiction of unknown lands, instead highlighting the impressive but explainable cartographic achievements of 16th-century mariners and mapmakers.

The Saqqara Bird, a small wooden artifact discovered in the tomb of the ancient Egyptian official Pa-di-Imen in Saqqara in 1898, has also been the subject of ancient astronaut speculation. The object, dating back to around 200 BCE, resembles a bird or a glider, leading some to suggest that it represents evidence of the ancient Egyptians' knowledge of aviation [20].

However, most Egyptologists believe that the Saqqara Bird was likely a ceremonial object or a toy, rather than a representation of an actual flying machine [21]. The ancient Egyptians are known to have made various wooden models and figurines for religious and funerary purposes, and the Saqqara Bird fits within this context [22].

Saqqara Bird — Wiki

In conclusion, while archaeological anomalies and artifacts that challenge our understanding of ancient technological capabilities are undeniably intriguing, they do not necessarily provide evidence of extraterrestrial intervention or lost advanced civilizations. It is essential to approach these findings with a critical and scientific mindset, considering the cultural, historical, and religious contexts in which they were created.

Many of the alleged advanced technologies found in mythological accounts, such as the vimanas in Hindu texts, are more likely the result of imaginative storytelling and the human fascination with the idea of flight, rather than descriptions of actual ancient aircraft. Similarly, artifacts like the Antikythera mechanism and the Baghdad Battery, while impressive and enigmatic, can be explained through the lens of human ingenuity and the accumulation of scientific knowledge over time.

The tendency to attribute unexplained or mysterious archaeological findings to extraterrestrial influence or lost advanced civilizations often stems from a misunderstanding of the capabilities and motivations of ancient cultures. By imposing modern technological expectations onto the past, we risk overlooking the remarkable achievements of our ancestors and the complex cultural and religious contexts in which they lived.

As we continue to explore the archaeological record and uncover new artifacts and sites that challenge our understanding of the past, it is crucial to maintain a balance between open-mindedness and scientific rigor. While some anomalies may remain unexplained or require further investigation, jumping to conclusions about alien intervention or lost advanced civilizations without substantial evidence can hinder our understanding of human history and cultural development.

In the end, the study of archaeological anomalies and their role in the ancient alien debate serves as a reminder of the enduring human fascination with the unknown and our desire to make sense of the world around us. By engaging with these mysteries through a critical and multidisciplinary approach, we can continue to expand our knowledge of the past and appreciate the incredible diversity and ingenuity of human cultures throughout history.

## References

[1] Jacobsen, K. A. (Ed.). (2011). *Brill's encyclopedia of Hinduism* (Vol. 3). Brill.

[2] Vālmīki, & Goldman, R. P. (2009). *The Rāmāyaṇa of Vālmīki: An epic of ancient India. Volume VI: Yuddhakāṇḍa.* Princeton University Press.

[3] Roy, P. C. (1889). *The Mahabharata of Krishna-Dwaipayana Vyasa.* Oriental Publishing Co.

[4] Feuerstein, G. (2002). *The yoga tradition: Its history, literature, philosophy and practice.* Motilal Banarsidass Publishers.

[5] Raman, B. V. (2005). *Variety in religion and science: Daily reflections.* iUniverse.

[6] Colavito, J. (2005). *The cult of alien gods: H.P. Lovecraft and extraterrestrial pop culture.* Prometheus Books.

[7] Freeth, T., et. al. (2006). Decoding the ancient Greek astronomical calculator known as the Antikythera Mechanism. *Nature, 444*(7119), 587-591.

[8] Marchant, J. (2010). *Decoding the heavens: A 2,000-year-old computer — and the century-long search to discover its secrets.* Da Capo Press.

[9] Edmunds, M. G. (2014). The Antikythera Mechanism and the mechanical universe. *Contemporary Physics, 55*(4), 263-285.

[10] Seiradakis, J. H., & Edmunds, M. G. (2018). Our current knowledge of the Antikythera Mechanism. *Nature Astronomy, 2,* 35–42. https://doi.org/10.1038/s41550-017-0347-2

[11] Mills, A. (2001). The 'Baghdad' battery. *Bulletin of the Scientific Instrument Society, 68,* 35-37

[12] Paszthory, E. (1989). Electricity generation or magic? The analysis of an unusual group of finds from Mesopotamia. *MASCA Research Papers in Science and Archaeology, 6,* 31-38.

[13] Eggert, G. (1996). The enigmatic 'Battery of Baghdad'. *Skeptical Inquirer, 20*(3), 31-34.

[14] Aveni, A. F. (2000). *Between the lines: The mystery of the giant ground drawings of ancient Nasca, Peru.* University of Texas Press.

[15] Reinhard, J. (1988). *The Nazca lines: A new perspective on their origin and meaning.* Editorial Los Pinos.

[16] Silverman, H. (1993). *Cahuachi in the ancient Nasca world.* University of Iowa Press.

[17] Kahle, P. (1956). The Piri Reis map (1513). *Imago Mundi, 13,* 54-55.

[18] McIntosh, G. C. (2000). *The Piri Reis map of 1513*. University of Georgia Press.

[19] Soucek, S. (1992). Islamic charting of the Mediterranean. In J. B. Harley & D. Woodward (Eds.), *The history of cartography, Volume 2, Book 1: Cartography in the traditional Islamic and South Asian societies* (pp. 263-292). University of Chicago Press.

[20] Verner, M. (2013). *Temple of the world: Sanctuaries, cults, and mysteries of ancient Egypt*. American University in Cairo Press.

[21] Hawass, Z. (2003). *The treasures of the pyramids*. American University in Cairo Press.

[22] Stevenson, A. (2009). *The Predynastic Egyptian cemetery of el-Gerzeh: Social identities and mortuary practices during the spread of the 'Naqada culture'* [Doctoral dissertation, University of Cambridge]. Apollo - University of Cambridge Repository. https://doi.org/10.17863/CAM.15920

# CHAPTER FOUR

## The rise of Homo sapiens: Creativity, adaptability and cognitive capabilities

*The human species is, as far as we know, the only species ever to have invented science, philosophy, music, art, and technology. We alone have devised systems of formal logic, geometry, physics, chemistry, biology. We alone have unraveled the structure of DNA, split the atom, discovered the Big Bang, and explained the origin of life itself.*

*Edward O. Wilson, The Meaning of Human Existence, 2014*

The history of Homo sapiens, spanning from our emergence in Africa around 300,000 years ago to the present day, is marked by countless examples of our species' creativity, adaptability, and ingenuity. Despite facing various challenges, including climate change and environmental pressures, Homo sapiens has consistently demonstrated its ability to innovate and thrive. This remarkable journey has led to the development of complex societies, advanced technologies, and a global civilization, all achieved through human intellect and perseverance.

Some key stages in the development of Homo sapiens include:

1. <u>Cognitive Revolution</u> (circa 70,000 to 30,000 years ago): This period is marked by the emergence of more complex language, art, and symbolic thinking. Evidence includes cave paintings, figurines, and advanced tool-making techniques.
2. <u>Upper Paleolithic Revolution</u> (circa 50,000 to 10,000 years ago): During this time, humans developed more sophisticated hunting tools, such as bows and arrows, and began to create more intricate and diverse forms of art and decoration
3. <u>Agricultural Revolution</u> (circa 10,000 years ago): The transition from hunter-gatherer societies to agricultural communities began around

10,000 years ago in various parts of the world. This shift had significant impacts on human culture, social structure, and technology.

4. <u>Urban Revolution</u> (circa 5,000 years ago): The development of cities and complex civilizations emerged in different regions, such as Mesopotamia, Egypt, and the Indus Valley. This period saw the rise of writing systems, centralized governments, and specialized occupations.

5. <u>Scientific and Industrial Revolutions</u> (circa 500 to 200 years ago): The Scientific Revolution, which began in the 16th century, laid the foundation for the Industrial Revolution in the 18th and 19th centuries. These periods were characterized by rapid advancements in science, technology, and manufacturing, which greatly impacted human society and culture.

6. <u>Digital Revolution</u> (late 20th century to present): The advent of digital technologies, such as computers and the internet, has transformed communication, information sharing, and various aspects of human life in recent decades.

Human development has progressed through these distinct stages, each marked by significant cultural and technological advances. These milestones reflect the gradual accumulation of knowledge and skills within Homo sapiens. Our cultural evolution continues to shape both our species and our world today, demonstrating the remarkable adaptability of human intelligence. This steady progression of human capabilities challenges notions of extraterrestrial intervention in our development.

One of the earliest demonstrations of human creativity can be observed in the African Middle Stone Age (300,000-50,000 years ago). During this period, Homo sapiens developed advanced stone tool technologies, such as the creation of blades and projectile points at the Kathu Pan 1 site in South Africa, dating back to around 500,000 years ago [1]. The use of symbolic materials, like the engraved ochre pieces found at Blombos Cave in South Africa, dating to around 75,000 years ago [2], and the shell beads discovered in Israel and

Algeria, dating to about 100,000 years ago [3], suggests the emergence of complex language and abstract thought.

As Homo sapiens spread across the globe, they encountered diverse environments and climate challenges. The Last Glacial Maximum, which occurred around 26,500 to 19,000 years ago, saw global temperatures drop and ice sheets expand, forcing human populations to adapt to new conditions [4]. Despite these challenges, human creativity flourished, as evidenced by the remarkable cave paintings at Lascaux in France and Altamira in Spain, dating back to around 17,000 and 36,000 years ago, respectively [5].

The invention of agriculture, which emerged independently in various regions between 10,000 and 4,000 years ago, was a turning point in human history. The Neolithic Revolution allowed for the growth of settled communities and the rise of complex civilizations. The ancient Sumerians in Mesopotamia developed the first known writing system, cuneiform, around 3500 BCE [6], while the ancient Egyptians constructed the Great Pyramid of Giza, one of the Seven Wonders of the Ancient World, around 2550 BCE [7].

The Olmec civilization, which flourished in Mesoamerica from about 1500 to 400 BCE, is known for creating impressive stone sculptures, such as the colossal heads weighing up to 50 tons [8]. The Maya civilization, which reached its peak between 250 and 900 CE, developed a sophisticated calendar system and built remarkable cities like Tikal and Copán [9].

The Inca Empire, which dominated the Andes region from 1438 to 1533 CE, is known for its incredible engineering feats, such as the construction of Machu Picchu, a city located at an altitude of 2,430 meters (9,7970 feet) [10]. The Inca also developed a complex system of roads, spanning over 40,000 kilometers (24,855 miles), that connected their vast empire [11].

The question of whether early Homo sapiens had the same cognitive capabilities as modern humans is a subject of ongoing research and debate in the scientific community. While the archaeological record provides evidence of human innovation, it's important to consider the cognitive capabilities that enabled these advancements.

One line of evidence comes from the study of brain size and structure. Fossil evidence indicates that Homo sapiens has had a brain size similar to that of modern humans for at least 300,000 years [12]. The cranial capacity of early Homo sapiens, such as the Jebel Irhoud fossils from Morocco dating back to around 315,000 years ago, falls within the range of modern human variation [13]. This suggests that the biological potential for modern human-like cognition was already present in early Homo sapiens.

Another important factor to consider is the archaeological evidence of complex behaviors and innovations associated with early Homo sapiens. The African Middle Stone Age (300,000-50,000 years ago) saw the emergence of advanced stone tool technologies, symbolic use of pigments, and the creation of personal ornaments [14, 15]. These developments are often interpreted as indicators of modern human-like cognition, including abstract thinking, planning, and social complexity.

Moreover, genetic studies have shown that modern humans and Neanderthals, our closest extinct relatives, interbred and produced fertile offspring [16]. This suggests that the cognitive differences between these species were likely not as profound as once thought.

However, it is essential to recognize that cognitive ability is not solely determined by brain size or genetic potential. Environmental, social, and cultural factors also play crucial roles in shaping human cognition and behavior [17]. The development of language, social learning, and cumulative culture allowed early Homo sapiens to build upon the knowledge and skills of previous generations, leading to the rapid advancement of technology and cultural complexity over time.

One of the key challenges to the alien astronaut idea is the significant time gap between the emergence of advanced societies in different parts of the world. The Sumerian civilization, often credited with the invention of writing and the building of the first ziggurats (stepped pyramidal structures), flourished in Mesopotamia from around 4500 BCE to 1900 BCE [18]. The Egyptian civilization, known for its iconic pyramids and rich mythology, rose to prominence around 3100 BCE and lasted until the Ptolemaic period ended in 30 BCE [19]. In contrast, the Mesoamerican civilizations, including the Olmecs, Mayas, and Aztecs, developed much later, with the earliest known pyramid, La Venta, dating to around 1000 BCE [20].

The following table shows the approximate years of existence for the major ancient civilizations that are connected with the ancient astronaut myth:

| Civilization | Period | Approximate Years |
|---|---|---|
| Sumerian | 4500 BCE – 1900 BCE | 2600 years |
| Ancient Egypt | 3100 BCE – 30 BCE | 3070 years |
| Indus Valley | 3300 BCE – 1300 BCE | 2000 years |
| Minoan | 3000 BCE – 1100 BCE | 1900 years |
| Olmec | 1500 BCE – 400 BCE | 1100 years |
| Assyrian | 1392 BCE – 609 BCE | 783 years |
| Phoenician | 1200 BCE – 539 BCE | 661 years |
| Ancient Greece | 1200 BCE – 146 BCE | 1054 years |
| Ancient Rome | 753 BCE – 476 CE | 1229 years |
| Nazca | 100 BCE – 800 CE | 900 years |
| Mayan (Classic Period) | 250 CE – 900 CE | 650 years |
| Toltec | 900 CE – 1168 CE | 268 years |
| Aztec | 1428 CE – 1521 CE | 93 years |
| Inca | 1438 CE – 1533 CE | 95 years |

The idea that extraterrestrial beings visited Earth and influenced human civilizations across a vast span of time, from Sumerian to Mesoamerican cultures, seems to strain credulity. The ancient astronaut theory is often presented in a way that implies a more concentrated period of alien intervention. These ideas tend to focus on specific artifacts, structures, or myths from various ancient cultures, presenting them as evidence of extraterrestrial influence without always providing clear dates or addressing the significant time gaps between the civilizations in question.

Cultural diffusion, the spread of ideas, technologies, and practices from one society to another, has played a significant role in shaping human history. While long-distance trade and communication networks in the ancient world were not as extensive as they are today, there is evidence of cultural exchange between distant regions. For example, the Silk Road, a network of trade routes connecting East Asia and the Mediterranean, facilitated the exchange of goods, ideas, and technologies between various civilizations from as early as the 2nd millennium BCE [21]. Similarly, maritime trade in the Indian Ocean and the Mediterranean Sea allowed for the spread of cultural influences between Africa, Asia, and Europe [22].

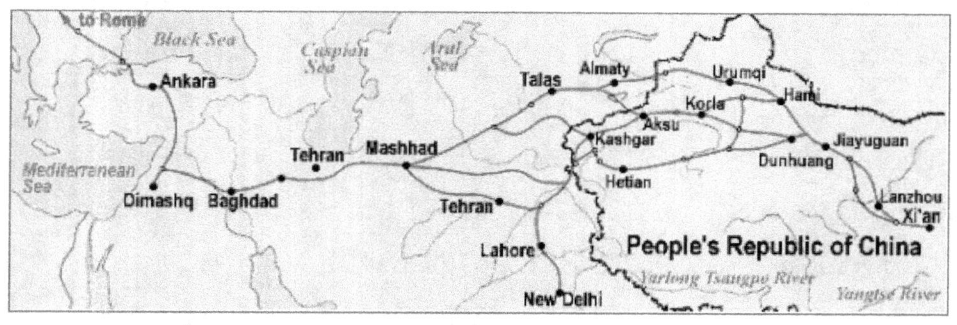


Ancient Silk Road— China Trekking

These trade networks not only facilitated the exchange of physical goods but also the transmission of ideas, stories, and religious beliefs. Merchants, travelers, and diplomats acted as conduits for the spread of cultural elements, carrying with them the knowledge and customs of their homelands. For example, the spread of Buddhism from India to Central and East Asia along the Silk Road demonstrates how religious ideas could travel vast distances and be adapted by different cultures [23].

However, it is important to recognize that cultural diffusion alone cannot account for all the similarities we observe in ancient civilizations. The concept of independent invention suggests that human beings, faced with similar challenges and equipped with comparable cognitive abilities, can arrive at similar solutions or ideas independently [24]. The development of agriculture, the invention of writing, and the creation of pyramidal structures are all examples of innovations that emerged separately in different parts of the world, likely driven by common human needs and desires.

The idea of independent invention is supported by the fact that we see similar developments occurring in geographically and temporally distinct cultures. For example, the concept of a supreme deity, a creator god responsible for the origin of the universe, is found in many ancient religions, from the Sumerian god Anu to the Egyptian god Atum and the Mayan god Itzamna [25]. While these deities may have different names and attributes, the underlying idea of a supreme creator is remarkably consistent across cultures.

Similarly, the use of pyramidal structures for religious or ceremonial purposes is not unique to Egypt and Mesoamerica. Pyramidal mounds and platforms have been found in various ancient cultures, such as the ziggurats of Mesopotamia, the stupas of ancient India, and the mound complexes of prehistoric North America [26]. The fact that these structures emerged independently in different parts of the world suggests that they were a response to common human impulses, such as the desire to create sacred spaces or to symbolically connect the earthly realm with the heavens.

Moreover, while there are indeed some striking similarities between the pyramids of Egypt and Mesoamerica, there are also significant differences in their design, construction techniques, and cultural significance. Egyptian pyramids were primarily built as tombs for pharaohs and were part of a complex funerary tradition [27], while Mesoamerican pyramids served as platforms for temples and were often associated with astronomical observations and ceremonial practices [28]. These differences suggest that the pyramid form may have arisen independently in these cultures, adapted to suit their specific beliefs and needs.

The same can be said for the similarities in mythological themes across ancient civilizations. While the presence of shared motifs, such as creation stories, flood myths, and tales of sky gods, is indeed intriguing, it does not necessarily imply direct alien influence. Many of these themes can be seen as expressions of universal human concerns and experiences, such as the desire to understand our origins, to be awe inspired by natural phenomena, and to fear catastrophic events.

For example, flood myths are found in numerous ancient cultures, from the Sumerian *Epic of Gilgamesh* to the Aztec story of the Great Flood and the biblical account of Noah's Ark [29]. While these stories differ in their specifics, they all share the basic idea of a catastrophic deluge that destroys the world, often as a form of divine punishment. The prevalence of flood myths across cultures may be attributed to the fact that many ancient societies developed in river valleys or coastal regions, where floods were a common and potentially devastating occurrence [30].

Similarly, the idea of celestial beings descending from the sky to interact with humans is a recurring theme in ancient mythologies. From the Sumerian god Enki, who imparted wisdom to humans, to the Mesoamerican feathered serpent deity Quetzalcoatl, who was said to have taught agriculture and the arts to humanity, these stories can be seen as metaphorical expressions of the human desire for divine knowledge and guidance [31]. The fact that similar themes appear in different cultures does not necessarily imply direct contact between them, but rather suggests that they are tapping into common human aspirations and fears.

Enki
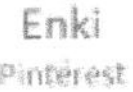
Pinterest

Quetzalcóatl
FreePik

# CHALLENGING THE ANCIENT ASTRONAUT MYTH

It is also worth noting that the ancient astronaut theory often relies on a selective and decontextualized reading of ancient texts and artifacts. Proponents of the theory tend to focus on specific elements that seem to resemble modern technology or space travel, while ignoring the broader cultural and religious context in which these elements appear. For example, the Sumerian King List, which mentions kings with extraordinarily long reigns, has been interpreted by some ancient astronaut theorists as evidence of extraterrestrial intervention [32]. However, this interpretation fails to consider the symbolic and political significance of these lengthy reigns, which were likely meant to convey the divine right and legitimacy of the kings rather than literal historical facts [33].

The concept of a Golden Age, a period of primordial harmony, prosperity, and enlightenment, is a common theme in the mythologies of various cultures worldwide. Many civilizations have stories of an advanced ancient society that existed in the far distant past, often associated with gods, demigods, or mythical rulers. Here are some examples:

## Greek mythology

In Greek myth, the Golden Age was the first of the five ages of mankind, a time of peace, harmony, and abundance under the rule of the titan Cronus. People lived long lives without strife or toil, and the earth provided food freely [34].

## Mesopotamian mythology

The *Sumerian King List*, an ancient text from Mesopotamia, describes a time before the great flood when gods and demigods ruled for extraordinarily long reigns, some lasting thousands of years [35]. This implies a golden age of divine rule and longevity.

## Hindu mythology

In Hindu cosmology, the universe goes through four cyclic ages or yugas. The first is the Satya Yuga or Krita Yuga, a golden age of truth, righteousness, and perfection, lasting 1,728,000 years [36]. Human beings were giants, lived for centuries, and possessed great knowledge and spiritual powers [37].

## Chinese mythology

In Chinese mythology, the era of the Three Sovereigns and Five Emperors, dating back to the 3rd millennium BCE, was considered a golden age of enlightened and virtuous rule [38]. These legendary sage-kings, such as the Yellow Emperor and Emperor Yao, were said to have brought prosperity, harmony, and advanced knowledge to ancient China [39].

## Aztec mythology

The Aztecs believed in a succession of five suns or ages, each ending in a catastrophe. The first age, known as 'Nahui-Ocelotl' (Jaguar Sun), was a time of giants and prosperity, but it was destroyed by jaguars [40].

## Norse mythology

In Norse myth, the Golden Age was associated with the realm of Ásgard, home of the gods. It was a time of peace, abundance, and the construction of great halls, such as Odin's Valhalla and the golden hall of Glaðsheimr [41].

## Atlantis (Greek Philosophy)

The story of Atlantis was first mentioned by the Greek philosopher Plato in his dialogues *Timaeus* and *Critias*, written around 360 BCE. According to Plato, Atlantis was a powerful and advanced island nation that existed 9,000 years before his time, which would place its existence around 9,600 BCE [42]. Plato described Atlantis as a utopian society that thrived during a golden age, but it ultimately fell out of favor with the gods and was destroyed by a cataclysmic flood or earthquake [43]. It's crucial to note that while Plato's dialogues are the only ancient sources that mention Atlantis, most scholars believe that the story is a philosophical allegory rather than a historical account [44].

Atlantis – AI generated—Quora

In the original mythological sources for these Golden Age narratives, there are no explicit mentions of ancient alien astronauts. The concept of extraterrestrial beings visiting Earth in the distant past and influencing human civilization is a modern idea that gained popularity in the mid-20th century.

However, some proponents of the ancient astronaut theory have reinterpreted these mythological stories through the lens of their beliefs. They suggest that the gods, demigods, and legendary figures described in these tales might have been advanced extraterrestrial beings who were misunderstood or mythologized by ancient humans.

For example, some ancient astronaut theorists have argued that the Sumerian gods in the King List, such as An, Enlil, and Enki, were actually alien visitors who ruled over early human civilization. Similarly, they have interpreted the long lifespans and supernatural abilities of figures in Hindu mythology, such as those in the Satya Yuga, as evidence of extraterrestrial intervention.

It is important to note that these interpretations are not supported by mainstream historians, archaeologists, or mythologists [45]. The ancient astronaut theory is considered a pseudoscientific concept that lacks convincing evidence and relies heavily on selective interpretation and speculation [46].

In summary, while the ancient astronaut theory attempts to explain the similarities in pyramid building and mythological themes across ancient civilizations by invoking extraterrestrial intervention, this view fails to account for the significant time gaps between these cultures and the complex processes of cultural diffusion and independent invention. The spread of ideas and technologies through trade networks, coupled with the human capacity for independent innovation, offers a more plausible explanation for these shared traits.

By recognizing the ingenuity and creativity of ancient human civilizations, we can appreciate the diverse ways in which our ancestors sought to understand and navigate the world around them, without resorting to speculative theories about alien influence. The similarities we observe in ancient cultures are a testament to the universality of human experience and the ability of our species to develop complex ideas and technologies independently, even in the face of vast geographical and temporal distances.

Rather than attributing these achievements to extraterrestrial intervention, we should celebrate the remarkable resilience and adaptability of ancient human societies, who developed sophisticated systems of knowledge and belief that allowed them to thrive in a wide range of environments and historical contexts. By studying these cultures on their own terms, and by seeking to understand the complex interplay of cultural diffusion and independent invention, we can gain a deeper appreciation for the richness and diversity of human history, and for the enduring legacy of our ancestors' intellectual and creative accomplishments.

As we continue to uncover new archaeological evidence and refine our understanding of ancient cultures, it becomes increasingly clear that the human capacity for innovation and adaptation is far more remarkable than any speculative theory of alien intervention. The achievements of our ancestors, from the development of agriculture to the construction of monumental architecture, are testaments to human ingenuity and perseverance.

Moreover, recognizing the independent achievements of diverse cultures around the world helps us to appreciate the value of cultural diversity and the multiple paths of human development. It challenges Eurocentric or other biased views of history and acknowledges the contributions of all human societies to our shared cultural heritage.

In conclusion, while the idea of ancient alien visitors may capture the imagination, the real story of human achievement is far more compelling. It is a story of countless generations of humans, facing challenges, solving problems, and gradually building the foundations of civilization through their own efforts and innovations. This narrative not only honors the achievements of our ancestors but also reminds us of our own potential for creativity and progress as we face the challenges of the present and future.

## References


[1] Wilkins, J., Schoville, B. J., Brown, K. S., & Chazan, M. (2012). Evidence for early hafted hunting technology. *Science, 338*(6109), 942-946.

[2] Henshilwood, C. S., et al. (2002). Emergence of modern human behavior: Middle stone age engravings from South Africa. *Science, 295*(5558), 1278-1280.

[3] Vanhaeren, M., d'Errico, F., Stringer, C., James, S. L., Todd, J. A., & Mienis, H. K. (2006). Middle Paleolithic shell beads in Israel and Algeria. *Science, 312*(5781), 1785-1788.

[4] Clark, P. U., et al. (2009). The Last Glacial Maximum. *Science, 325*(5941), 710-714.

[5] Valladas, H., et al. (2001). Palaeolithic paintings: Evolution of prehistoric cave art. *Nature, 413*(6855), 479.

[6] Kramer, S. N. (1963). *The Sumerians: Their history, culture, and character.* University of Chicago Press.

[7] Lehner, M. (1997). *The complete pyramids.* Thames & Hudson.

[8] Diehl, R. A. (2004). *The Olmecs: America's first civilization*. Thames & Hudson.

[9] Sharer, R. J., & Traxler, L. P. (2006). *The ancient Maya* (6th ed.). Stanford University Press.

[10] Burger, R. L., & Salazar, L. C. (Eds.). (2004). *Machu Picchu: Unveiling the mystery of the Incas*. Yale University Press.

[11] D'Altroy, T. N. (2002). *The Incas*. Blackwell Publishers.

[12] Neubauer, S., Hublin, J. J., & Gunz, P. (2018). The evolution of modern human brain shape. *Science Advances*, *4*(1), Article eaao5961.

[13] Hublin, J. J., et al. (2017). New fossils from Jebel Irhoud, Morocco and the pan-African origin of Homo sapiens. *Nature*, *546*(7657), 289-292.

[14] McBrearty, S., & Brooks, A. S. (2000). The revolution that wasn't: A new interpretation of the origin of modern human behavior. *Journal of Human Evolution*, *39*(5), 453-563.

[15] Henshilwood, C. S., et al. (2002). Emergence of modern human behavior: Middle stone age engravings from South Africa. *Science*, *295*(5558), 1278-1280.

[16] Green, R. E., et al. (2010). A draft sequence of the Neandertal genome. *Science*, *328*(5979), 710-722.

[17] Heyes, C. (2012). New thinking: The evolution of human cognition. *Philosophical Transactions of the Royal Society B: Biological Sciences*, *367*(1599), 2091-2096.

[18] Kramer, S. N. (1963). *The Sumerians: Their history, culture, and character*. University of Chicago Press.

[19] Shaw, I. (Ed.). (2000). *The Oxford history of ancient Egypt*. Oxford University Press.

[20] Grove, D. C., & Gillespie, S. D. (1992). Ideology and evolution at the pre-state level: Formative period Mesoamerica. In A. A. Demarest & G. W. Conrad (Eds.), *Ideology and pre-Columbian civilizations* (pp. 15-36). School of American Research Press.

[21] Liu, X. (2010). *The Silk Road in world history*. Oxford University Press.

[22] Beaujard, P. (2005). The Indian Ocean in Eurasian and African world-systems before the sixteenth century. *Journal of World History, 16*(4), 411-465.

[23] Foltz, R. (2010). *Religions of the Silk Road: Premodern patterns of globalization*. Palgrave Macmillan.

[24] Merton, R. K. (1973). *The sociology of science: Theoretical and empirical investigations*. University of Chicago Press.

[25] Leeming, D. A. (2010). *Creation myths of the world: An encyclopedia*. ABC-CLIO.

[26] Trigger, B. G. (1990). Monumental architecture: A thermodynamic explanation of symbolic behaviour. *World Archaeology, 22*(2), 119-132.

[27] Lehner, M. (1997). *The complete pyramids: Solving the ancient mysteries*. Thames and Hudson.

[28] Aveni, A. F. (2001). *Skywatchers: A revised and updated version of Skywatchers of ancient Mexico*. University of Texas Press.

[29] Dundes, A. (Ed.). (1988). *The flood myth*. University of California Press.

[30] Witzel, M. (2012). *The origins of the world's mythologies*. Oxford University Press.

[31] Miller, M. E., & Taube, K. (1993). *The gods and symbols of ancient Mexico and the Maya: An illustrated dictionary of Mesoamerican religion*. Thames and Hudson.

[32] Michalowski, P. (1983). History as charter: Some observations on the Sumerian King List. *Journal of the American Oriental Society, 103*(1), 237-248.

[33] Jacobsen, T. (1939). *The Sumerian King List*. University of Chicago Press.

[34] Hesiod. (1914). *Works and days* (H. G. Evelyn-White, Trans.). Harvard University Press.

[35] Jacobsen, T. (1939). *The Sumerian King List*. University of Chicago Press.

[36] González-Reimann, L. (2002). *The Mahābhārata and the Yugas: India's great epic poem and the Hindu system of world ages*. Peter Lang.

[37] Zimmer, H. (1972). *Myths and symbols in Indian art and civilization*. Princeton University Press.

[38] Birrell, A. (1999). *Chinese mythology: An introduction*. Johns Hopkins University Press.

[39] Sima, Q. (1993). *Records of the Grand Historian: Qin Dynasty* (B. Watson, Trans.). Columbia University Press.

[40] Taube, K. (1993). *Aztec and Maya myths*. University of Texas Press.

[41] Lindow, J. (2002). *Norse mythology: A guide to gods, heroes, rituals, and beliefs*. Oxford University Press.

[42] Plato. (1929). *Timaeus and Critias* (A. E. Taylor, Trans.). Routledge.

[43] Ellis, R. (1999). *Imagining Atlantis*. Vintage.

[44] Vidal-Naquet, P. (1986). *The Atlantis story: A short history of Plato's myth*. University of Exeter Press.

[45] Feder, K. L. (2020). *Encyclopedia of dubious archaeology: From Atlantis to the Walam Olum*. Greenwood Press.

[46] Harrold, F. B., & Eve, R. A. (1987). *Cult archaeology and creationism: Understanding pseudoscientific beliefs about the past*. University of Iowa Press.

# CHAPTER FIVE

# Misinterpreting the myths: How the ancient astronaut theory distorts the past

—————

*One of the most interesting and perplexing aspects of ancient mythology is the consistent appearance of gods descending from the heavens in chariots of fire. The vivid descriptions of these divine vehicles have inspired speculation and reinterpretation over the centuries, leading some to wonder if these myths could be ancient accounts of extraterrestrial visitations.*

*Carl Sagan, The Cosmic Connection: An Extraterrestrial Perspective, 1973.*

For adherents of the ancient astronaut theory, the prevalence of anomalous descriptions and depictions across the mythologies, folklore, and sacred texts of the world's earliest civilizations seems tantalizing. To these believers, such references represent tangible records of prehistoric extraterrestrial encounters and interventions [1].

Proponents of the ancient astronaut hypothesis often project fantastic propositions onto ambiguous primordial stories, artworks, and writings. In their zeal to substantiate fringe beliefs, passages, symbols, and iconography get contorted into corroborating 'ancient alien evidence' through fanciful reinterpretations decontextualized from the original sources [2]:

- Outlandish beings descending from the skies in blazing chariots or spacecraft.
- Metaphysical conveyances equating to cutting-edge technologies bestowed by enlightened star-people upon ancient humans just gaining self-awareness.
- Abundant hints of advanced godlike entities kickstarting agriculture, creation myths, and even the construction of megalithic wonders for our ancestors through teaching and subtle genetic uplifting.

The following table summarizes various human civilizations from the Upper Paleolithic period onward that had myths or folklore that some have interpreted as being about extraterrestrial beings visiting Earth:

| Archeological period | Years (approx.) | Civilization | Myths about extraterrestrials |
| --- | --- | --- | --- |
| Upper Paleolithic (Old Stone Age) | 50,000 - 10,000 BCE | Various hunter-gatherer groups | Cave paintings and petroglyphs like those in Valcamonica and Tassili n'Ajjer depict strange beings, interpreted by some as alien astronauts. |
| Neolithic (New Stone Age) | 10,000 - 2,000 BCE | Various early agricultural societies | The Dogon tribe of Mali have myths about the Nommo, amphibious beings from the Sirius star system. |
| Bronze Age | 3,300 - 1,200 BCE | Sumerians | Sumerian texts mention the Anunnaki, deities whom some suggest were extraterrestrials. |
| | | Ancient Egyptians | Pyramid texts and the mythology of gods like Ra and Thoth have been interpreted by some as referencing alien visitors. |
| *Iron Age* | *1,200 BCE - 600 CE* | Ancient Greeks | Myths of gods visiting from the heavens, such as the story of Prometheus bringing fire, have been linked to ancient astronauts. |
| | | Judeo-Christian *Bible* | Biblical references to 'Nephilim', 'Elohim' and flying chariots have been interpreted by some as accounts of ancient astronauts. |
| | | Indian Vedic Period | Ancient texts like the Rigveda and the Mahabharata mention mythical flying machines that some have suggested relate to ancient astronauts. |

# CHALLENGING THE ANCIENT ASTRONAUT MYTH

## Upper Paleolithic Period (50,000 BCE to 10,000 BCE)

Some believe the myths of ancient alien astronauts have origins stretching back to the Upper Paleolithic period, when early humans created cave paintings and petroglyphs depicting mysterious, otherworldly beings and objects, as seen in Valcamonica, Italy, and Tassili n'Ajjer, Algeria. These ancient artworks are interpreted by some as evidence of extraterrestrial contact, suggesting early humans might have been visited or influenced by advanced beings from other worlds [3].

The Valcamonica petroglyphs show anthropomorphic figures with shining helmets and two tools in their hands—a straight one and a three-pointed one. These images resemble similar ones found in South America, Egypt, Australia, India, and Sumeria, linking them to gods such as Viracocha, Zeus, Baal, and others.

Most archaeologists and historians do not support the 'alien astronauts' interpretation, considering the depictions to be symbolic or representative of shamanistic practices, deities, or mythological figures relevant to the culture and period of the people who created them [4].

The Valcamonica 'alien astronauts' — Circa 3,000 BCE— Wikipedia

As humanity transitioned through the Neolithic, Bronze, and Iron Ages, these speculative interpretations continued to evolve. The Neolithic period saw the rise of complex societies and monumental architecture, such as the megalithic structures at Göbekli Tepe and Stonehenge, which some suggest were constructed with the guidance of extraterrestrial visitors. In the Bronze Age, civilizations like the Sumerians and Egyptians recorded their myths and histories in texts and artifacts, leading to interpretations of gods like the Anunnaki and deities of the Egyptian pantheon as potential alien beings. Finally, the Iron Age, particularly during the Vedic Period in ancient India, introduced concepts such as vimanas—mythical flying machines mentioned in the Mahabharata and other texts—that have been linked by some to advanced extraterrestrial technology [5]. These ancient myths and artifacts, when viewed through the lens of ancient astronaut theories, weave a narrative of possible alien influence throughout human history.

## Neolithic Period (10,000 BCE to 2,000 BCE)

The Neolithic Period was marked by significant advancements in human society, including the development of agriculture, permanent settlements, and the creation of complex tools and pottery [6].

During this period, sites such as Stonehenge in England, Göbekli Tepe in Turkey, and the pyramids of Egypt are often pointed to as evidence of alien influence due to their impressive construction and alignment with astronomical phenomena. Mainstream archaeology attributes these achievements to the ingenuity, engineering skills, and social organization of early human societies. Stories of gods, sky beings, and otherworldly visitors are often interpreted by ancient alien theorists as descriptions of extraterrestrial contact. Scholars typically view these as mythological or religious narratives that reflect the beliefs and imagination of the cultures that created them [7].

## Bronze Age (Approx 3300 BCE to 1200 BCE)

The transition from the Neolithic to the Bronze Age marks a significant advancement in human technology with the widespread use of bronze (an alloy of copper and tin) and social organization with the rise of early cities and urban centers. The major communities in the Bronze Age were:

<u>Mesopotamia (Sumeria, Akkad, Babylonia, and Assyria)</u>

Key developments include the establishment of city-states, the creation of cuneiform writing, and the construction of monumental structures like ziggurats [8].

Few mythological sources have been more exploited by ancient astronaut theorists than the ancient Sumerians' creation myths, hero tales, and cuneiform writings. Some authors have presented hypotheses that the Sumerian gods such as Anu, Enlil, and Enki were actually representatives of an alien race known as the 'Anunnaki' who came to Earth from another planet to mine gold and initiate the creation of the human race.

Despite containing no references to aliens, planets, genetics, or mining operations, these interpretations of Sumerian texts have nonetheless inspired many to perceive the Anunnaki as cosmic ancestors uplifting early man rather than symbolic deities [9]. These creative 'translations' of gods traveling in sun-like celestial chariots as depictions of ancient aircraft and journeys from other worlds sparked a pop culture obsession.

Akkadian cylinder seal depicting members of the Annunaki (Inanna, Utu and Enki))— Circa 2300 BCE—Wikipedia

Similarly, obscure references to 'vimanas' (flying objects or antimatter burners) from ancient Indian texts like the Vedas and Sanskrit epics have been interpreted by some authors as purported evidence of prehistoric aeronautical or even nuclear technologies imparted by alien teachers [10]. However, the actual context of the vimana typically equates to poetic metaphysical symbolism being co-opted into literal re-imaginings completely unsupported by fact-based translations or primary sources. This pattern of misinterpretation extends to other ancient cultures as well.

<u>Mesoamerican and Andean Civilizations</u>

Various civilizations in South America have become associated with ancient alien astronaut theories. These are:

- Caral-Supe Civilization (Circa 3000 BCE – 1800 BCE)

Located in the Supe Valley of present-day Peru, it is one of the oldest known civilizations in the Americas, dating back to around 3000

BCE. It is notable for its large pyramidal structures, sophisticated urban planning, and early use of irrigation agriculture. From the perspective of ancient astronaut theories, the monumental architecture and the sudden appearance of complex society are often highlighted, with proponents suggesting that extraterrestrial beings might have influenced their development, although mainstream archaeology attributes these advancements to human innovation [11].

- Olmec Civilization (Circa 1500 BCE – 400 BCE)

The Olmec Civilization, flourishing between approximately 1500 BCE and 400 BCE in the Gulf Coast region of Mexico, is often considered the 'mother culture' of Mesoamerica. The Olmecs are renowned for their colossal stone heads, intricate art, and early forms of writing and calendrical systems. Ancient astronaut theorists often point to the Olmec heads, with their unique facial features, as possible evidence of extraterrestrial visitors. The sophistication of their societal structures and their mysterious origins also fuel speculation, though scholars emphasize the Olmecs' foundational influence on later Mesoamerican cultures [12].

Olmec stone head—Pixabay: mochilazocultural

- Mayan Civilization (Circa 2000 BCE - 16th Century CE)

The Mayan Civilization, which reached its peak between 250 CE and 900 CE, spanned present-day Mexico, Belize, Guatemala, Honduras, and El Salvador. The Mayans are celebrated for their advanced writing system, complex calendar, and impressive architectural achievements, including pyramids, palaces, and observatories. Proponents of ancient astronaut theories often cite the Mayan's detailed astronomical knowledge and the precision of their calendar as indicators of alien influence. Additionally, some interpret certain Mayan artworks and carvings as depictions of extraterrestrial beings or spacecraft. However, archaeologists attribute these accomplishments to the Mayan's extensive scientific and mathematical knowledge [13].

# CHALLENGING THE ANCIENT ASTRONAUT MYTH

A prime example is the frequent citing of the Mayan book known as the *Popol Vuh* by ancient alienists. Its creation myths jam-packed with symbolism and metaphors involving celestial beings and trials regularly get imposed as literal transcripts chronicling alien visitations directing the beginning and development of Mayan civilization [14].

- Nazca Civilization (Circa 100 BCE – 800 CE)

The Nazca Civilization thrived between 100 BCE and 800 CE in the southern coastal region of Peru. They are most famous for the Nazca Lines, enormous geoglyphs etched into the desert, depicting various animals, plants, and geometric shapes. Ancient astronaut theorists suggest that these lines could have served as landing strips or signals for extraterrestrial spacecraft, given their visibility from the air. Mainstream interpretations, however, focus on their possible ceremonial or astronomical purposes, created by human ingenuity using simple tools and methods [15].

- Teotihuacan Civilization (Circa 100 BCE – 550 BCE)

The Teotihuacan Civilization, which existed from around 100 BCE to 550 CE near modern-day Mexico City, was one of the largest cities in the ancient world. It is renowned for its massive pyramids, such as the Pyramid of the Sun and the Pyramid of the Moon, and its well-planned urban grid. Ancient astronaut enthusiasts often speculate that the scale and precision of Teotihuacan's architecture, as well as its astronomical alignments, might indicate alien influence or guidance. However, archaeologists credit these feats to the sophisticated engineering and organizational skills of its inhabitants [16].

Pyramid of the Sun, Teotihuacan—Wikimedia

- Aztec Civilization (Circa 1345 CE – 1521 CE)

The Aztec Civilization, flourishing from the early 14th century until the Spanish conquest in 1521, established a powerful empire in central Mexico with their capital at Tenochtitlan (now Mexico City). The Aztecs are known for their complex social, political, and religious systems, as well as their impressive architectural accomplishments. Ancient astronaut theorists sometimes point to the Aztec myths of gods descending from the sky as potential evidence of extraterrestrial contact. They also highlight the advanced construction techniques and the grand scale of Aztec temples and pyramids. Mainstream scholarship, however, attributes these to the Aztecs' well-developed societal organization and architectural knowledge [17].

- Inca Civilization (Circa 1400 CE – 1533 CE)

The Inca Civilization, the largest empire in pre-Columbian America, flourished from the early 15th century until the Spanish conquest in

1533. Centered in the Andean region of South America, the Incas are known for their sophisticated road systems, agricultural terraces, and iconic sites like Machu Picchu and Cusco. Ancient astronaut theorists often highlight the precision of Inca stonework, such as the fitting of massive stones without mortar, as possible evidence of advanced or extraterrestrial technology. They also point to the legends of the Inca gods, who were said to have come from the sky, as potential indications of alien influence. Archaeologists, however, attribute these achievements to the Incas' advanced engineering and organizational skills [18].

## Summarizing the Mesoamerican and Andean Findings

The ancient astronaut theories suggest that extraterrestrial beings visited Earth and influenced human civilizations, but applying this idea to the diverse and extensive range of Mesoamerican and Andean civilizations presents significant challenges. These civilizations span thousands of years, from the Caral-Supe civilization around 3000 BCE to the Inca civilization's height in the 16th century CE. They were spread across vast and varied regions, each developing unique technological, architectural, and societal achievements. The immense temporal scope and geographical diversity make it difficult to attribute a single external influence to all these cultures [19].

Proponents of ancient astronaut theories often point to impressive architectural achievements, sophisticated astronomical knowledge, and mysterious artifacts as evidence of extraterrestrial contact. For instance, the precision of Inca stonework, the Nazca Lines' large geoglyphs, and the Maya's detailed calendars and astronomy are cited as possible indicators of alien influence. However, mainstream archaeology attributes these achievements to human ingenuity, gradual technological progress, and cultural exchanges, dismissing the need for external intervention [20].

Moreover, the lack of consistent, direct evidence linking these civilizations to extraterrestrial visitors weakens the ancient astronaut hypothesis. Many of the so-called 'alien' artifacts and symbols can be explained through cultural context and symbolism intrinsic to these societies. Interpretations of these items often overlook the rich mythological and religious frameworks that shaped their creation. The idea of extraterrestrials influencing multiple, widely separated civilizations over millennia also raises questions about the nature and objectives of such hypothetical contact [21].

While the ancient astronaut theories provide an intriguing speculative narrative, they fail to account for the independent, context-specific developments of Mesoamerican and Andean civilizations. The remarkable achievements of these societies are best understood through the lens of human creativity, adaptation, and cultural evolution. The archaeological evidence supports a view of these civilizations as products of human innovation, influenced by their unique environments and interactions, rather than by external extraterrestrial forces [22].

## Australian Aboriginal rock art (Circa 28,000 BCE)

Most Australian rock art has been dated to around 28,000 BCE, although there are possibly much older sites on the continent. Some sites depict figures with halos around their heads, and these images have specific cultural and symbolic meanings that are deeply rooted in Aboriginality and cosmology. They reflect human creativity, religious beliefs, and social structures rather than encounters with extraterrestrial beings.

Some figures are known as 'Dreamtime' figures with the halos signifying their sacred and powerful nature. Other halos may represent the spiritual power or sacred knowledge possessed by these beings. Understanding these images requires a respect for and knowledge of the cultural and spiritual context in which they were created [23, 24].

Here are a few examples:

### The Wandjina

The Wandjina are cloud and rain spirits in the mythology of several Aboriginal groups in northern Australia, particularly the Mowanjum people. They are depicted in rock art as large anthropomorphic figures with round, white faces, large black eyes, and no mouths. Some alien astronaut theorists have claimed the Wandjina represent alien visitors wearing helmets or spacesuits. However, in Aboriginal traditions they are sacred creation beings associated with weather and seasonal change, not aliens.

## The Bradshaw rock paintings

Also known as Gwion art, these enigmatic red ochre paintings in the Kimberley region of Western Australia depict stick-like human figures in elaborate costumes or bodily adornment. Some of the figures have been interpreted as wearing spacesuits, helmets, antennae, etc. However, archaeologists see this simply as a distinct artistic style of representing the human form, with no evidence that they depict anything extraterrestrial.

Gwion figures wearing ornate costumes—Wikipedia

## The Baiame story

Baiame is a creator god in the mythology of several Aboriginal groups in southeastern Australia. In some stories, Baiame is said to have come down from the sky to the top of a mountain and created the first humans. While some have tried to interpret this through an ancient astronaut lens, the story is a

Dreamtime creation myth, with Baiame clearly a spiritual creator being, not an alien.

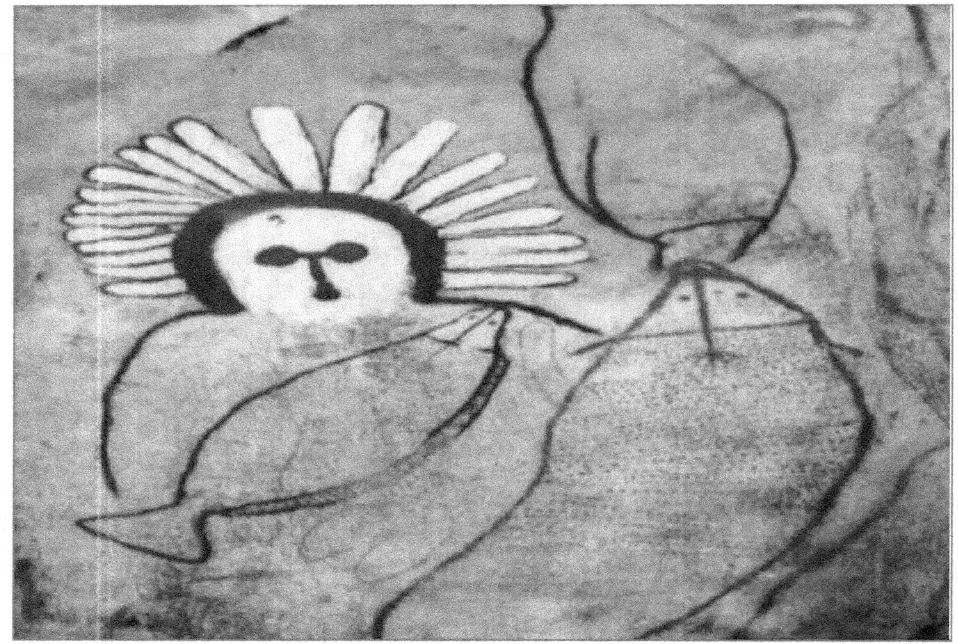

Australian Aboriginal Rock Art — The Wandjina (Ancestor Beings) — Trip Dog

Aboriginal elders and communities object to fringe 'alien' interpretations of their sacred stories and artwork. The mythological elements are much better understood in terms of Aboriginal cosmology and worldviews, not modern alien astronaut beliefs anachronistically projected onto ancient cultures [25-27]. The mainstream scholarly view is that there is no convincing evidence linking Aboriginal traditions to alien contact [28-30].

The misinterpretation of Australian Aboriginal rock art by ancient astronaut theorists follows a similar pattern to that seen with other ancient art forms discussed earlier. Just as the Valcamonica petroglyphs in Italy or the Nazca Lines in Peru have been misconstrued as depictions of alien visitors, the Wandjina and other Aboriginal figures have been subject to similar speculative interpretations. This parallel misinterpretation across diverse cultures and time periods highlights a common tendency among ancient astronaut theorists to project modern, technologically-influenced ideas onto ancient symbolic art, disregarding the rich cultural context in which these artworks were created.

## Forged artifacts and hoaxed texts

Beyond the misappropriation of genuine ancient myths and artwork, the zeal to prove prehistoric extraterrestrial intervention has also incentivized the outright fabrication of archaeological evidence. Sensational claims about the Kentril Tablets, Burrows Cave writings, and the Constantinean Donation exemplify how manufactured antiquities or Medieval forgeries get wielded to rewrite conventional history.

These hoaxes rely on couching their extraordinary 'revelations' in the hazy origins of primordial civilizations or gaps in the textual record. The Kentril artifacts, supposedly proving trans-oceanic contact and advanced astronomical knowledge in ancient Phoenician times, were swiftly unmasked as amateurish fakes once subjected to rudimentary analysis [31].

Similarly, the allegedly 4000-year-old Burrows Cave Tablets bearing inscriptions in a hieroglyphic writing system predating all others collapsed under basic dating techniques and identification of the stone as recently quarried [32]. The texts themselves devolved into meaningless pseudoscientific word salads under linguistic scrutiny.

More insidiously, ideologically-motivated fabrications like The Constantinean Donation managed to get upheld as factual for centuries by institutions invested in its narrative of bestowed authority, despite blatant authenticity issues [35]. Its longevity demonstrates the stubborn appeal of manufactured ancient artifacts — even when overwhelmingly exposed as disinformation.

Modern archaeological techniques have played a crucial role in debunking many ancient astronaut claims. Advanced dating methods, such as radiocarbon dating and thermoluminescence, have provided more accurate timelines for artifacts and structures, often contradicting the chronologies proposed by ancient astronaut theorists. For instance, these techniques have confirmed that the Egyptian pyramids were indeed built during the Old Kingdom period, refuting claims of much earlier, alien-assisted construction.

Furthermore, geophysical survey methods like ground-penetrating radar and LiDAR (Light Detection and Ranging) have revealed the methods used in constructing ancient monuments without the need for extraterrestrial intervention. These technologies have shown how earthworks like the Nazca Lines could have been created using simple tools and surveying techniques available to ancient peoples. Similarly, microscopic analysis of stone tools and cut marks on megalithic structures has demonstrated the use of period-appropriate technologies, countering claims of advanced alien tools.

Lastly, interdisciplinary approaches combining archaeology with anthropology, linguistics, and cognitive science have provided more nuanced understandings of ancient myths and symbols. This holistic approach has shown how supposedly 'alien' narratives in ancient texts can be better explained as metaphorical expressions of natural phenomena or complex philosophical concepts within their cultural contexts. These scientific advancements have consistently reinforced the ingenuity and capabilities of our human ancestors, undermining the need for extraterrestrial explanations.

More recently, a rash of 'Black World Order' forgeries pandering to fringe theories with incendiary alternative history claims, and hoax 'Sumerian seals' embellished with anachronistic alien imagery, continue stoking the public fascination for ancient astronaut evidence [34]. Demarcating the line between documenting actual prehistoric cultural records like Native American legends and enabling modern myth-making remains a pressing issue [35].

Ultimately, the academic rigor of verifying provenance, pursuing radiometric and chemical testing, and maintaining authentication standards offers the strongest bulwark against these recurring waves of pseudo archaeology. Fraudulent artifacts and manuscripts will undoubtedly continue to emerge so long as there is a motivated audience for their 'paradigm-shifting' narratives.

### The myths of our myths

What these diverse examples cumulatively showcase is the insidious manner by which symbolic tales and artwork from our ancient ancestors routinely become fertile hunting grounds for perpetuating fringe extraterrestrial folklore and pseudo histories. With self-reinforcing speculation congealing into popular mythological narratives, every ambiguous cultural reference, descriptive flourish, or contextual unknown surrounding ancient texts gets filled in with sensationalized ancient astronaut propositions.Apocryphal stories turn into eyewitness accounts. Metaphoric imagery is reduced to literal interstellar encounters. The very human practice of rich storytelling to enshrine existential mysteries and cultural traditions becomes reprocessed into Sci-Fi fictional chronicles posing as historical records. Judeo-Christian and Hindu deities become misidentified as direct manifestations of alien entities guiding our civilization [36].

While enthusiastic claims about physically representing ancient texts and artworks remain unverified and widely derided by scholars across virtually all relevant academic disciplines, little objective rigor is applied to even contextually assessing source descriptions before proclaiming them long-lost documentation about our extraterrestrial benefactors [33, 34].

More critically, we see how such literal interpretations uphold latent supremacist and Eurocentric biases — denying the ingenuity and self-determination demonstrated by ancient societies as being able to develop sophisticated cosmologies in harmony with their indigenous experiences and natural world observations. Why default to injecting an alien deus ex machina explanation unless one subconsciously subscribes to a patronizing perspective that our ancestors were too primitive to independently cultivate symbolic myth, art and technology? Accepting ancient peoples as equally sentient and intelligent banishes the need to superimpose fanciful celestial intervention onto their realms of knowledge [19, 20].

## References

[1] Colavito, J. (2005). *The cult of alien gods: H.P. Lovecraft and extraterrestrial pop culture.* Prometheus Books.

[2] Fritze, R. H. (2009). *Invented knowledge: False history, fake science and pseudo-religions.* Reaktion Books.

[3] Anati, E. (2004). *Valcamonica rock art: A new history for Europe*. Centro Camuno di Studi Preistorici.

[4] Haughton, B. (2007). *Hidden history: Lost civilizations, secret knowledge, and ancient mysteries*. New Page Books.

[5] Bellwood, P. (2004). *First farmers: The origins of agricultural societies*. Wiley-Blackwell.

[6] Fagan, B. M. (2001). *The seventy great mysteries of the ancient world: Unlocking the secrets of past civilizations*. Thames & Hudson.

[7] Kramer, S. N. (1963). *The Sumerians: Their history, culture, and character*. University of Chicago Press.

[8] Heiser, M. S. (2017). *The unseen realm: Recovering the supernatural worldview of the Bible*. Lexham Press.

[9] Shady, R., Haas, J., & Creamer, W. (2001). Dating Caral, a preceramic site in the Supe Valley on the central coast of Peru. *Science, 292*(5517), 723-726.

[10] Diehl, R. A. (2004). *The Olmecs: America's first civilization*. Thames & Hudson.

[11] Coe, M. D. (2011). *The Maya* (8th ed.). Thames & Hudson.

[12] Tedlock, D. (1996). *Popol Vuh: The Mayan book of the dawn of life and the glories of gods and kings*. Simon and Schuster.

[13] Aveni, A. F. (2000). *Between the lines: The mystery of the giant ground drawings of ancient Nasca, Peru*. University of Texas Press.

[14] Cowgill, G. L. (2015). *Ancient Teotihuacan: Early urbanism in central Mexico*. Cambridge University Press.

[15] Smith, M. E. (2012). *The Aztecs* (3rd ed.). Wiley-Blackwell.

[16] D'Altroy, T. N. (2002). *The Incas*. Wiley-Blackwell.

[17] Fagan, B. M. (2004). *The seventy great mysteries of the ancient world: Unlocking the secrets of past civilizations.* Thames & Hudson.

[18] Feder, K. L. (2020). *Frauds, myths, and mysteries: Science and pseudoscience in archaeology* (10th ed.). Oxford University Press.

[19] Fagan, G. G. (Ed.). (2006). *Archaeological fantasies: How pseudoarchaeology misrepresents the past and misleads the public.* Routledge.

[20] Díaz-Andreu, M. (2005). Recent studies in rock art: Review article. *American Journal of Archaeology, 107,* 107-110.

[21] Morphy, H. (1999). Traditional and modern visual art of hunting and gathering peoples. In R. B. Lee & R. Daly (Eds.), *The Cambridge encyclopedia of hunters and gatherers* (pp. 441-448). Cambridge University Press.

[22] Porr, M., & Bell, H. R. (2012). 'Rock-art', 'animism' and two-way thinking: Towards a complementary epistemology in the understanding of material culture and 'rock-art' of hunting and gathering people. *Journal of Archaeological Method and Theory, 19*(1), 161-205.

[23] Donaldson, M. (2009). Wandjina, graffiti and heritage: The power and politics of enduring imagery. *Humanities Research, 15*(2), 153-183.

[24] Welch, D. (2016). *From Bradshaw to Wandjina Australian Aboriginal Culture Series No. 12: Aboriginal paintings of the Kimberley, Western Australia.* David Welch Publications.

[25] Elkin, A. P. (1974). *The Australian Aborigines* (5th ed.). Angus & Robertson Publishers.

[26] Feder, K. L. (2021). *Frauds, myths, and mysteries: Science and pseudoscience in archaeology* (9th ed.). Oxford University Press.

[27] Smith, C., & Burke, H. (2007). *Digging it up down under: A practical guide to doing archaeology in Australia.* Springer.

[28] Michel, C., & Friedrich, M. (2020). Fakes and forgeries of written artefacts: An introduction. In *Fakes and forgeries of written artefacts from ancient Mesopotamia to modern China* (pp. 1-22). De Gruyter.

[29] Wilson, J. (2012). The cave who never was: Outsider archaeology and failed collaboration in the USA. *Public Archaeology, 11*(2), 73-95.

[30] Valla, L. (2007). *On the Donation of Constantine* (C. B. Coleman, Trans.). Harvard University Press. (Original work published 1440.)

[31] Coppens, P. (2010). *The new pyramid age: Worldwide discoveries of new pyramids challenge our thinking*. Axis Mundi Books.

[32] Newman, A. (2010). The Walam Olum: An indigenous apocrypha and its readers. *American Literary History, 22*(1), 26-56.

[33] Feder, K. L. (2020). *Frauds, myths, and mysteries: Science and pseudoscience in archaeology* (10th ed.). Oxford University Press.

[34] Fagan, G. G. (Ed.). (2006). *Archaeological fantasies: How pseudoarchaeology misrepresents the past and misleads the public*. Routledge.

# CHAPTER SIX
## Aliens in ancient religious texts and art

———

*The gods of myth and legend are not aliens who visited earth in ancient times in space ships. They are the creations of the human imagination, shaped by the cultures and experiences of the people who invented them. To interpret them otherwise is to misunderstand their meaning and their power.*

*Dr. Kenneth L. Fede, 2020.*

*Frauds, Myths, and Mysteries: Science and Pseudoscience in Archaeology (10th ed.).*

One of the central pillars of the ancient astronaut theory is the claim that evidence for extraterrestrial intervention can be found in the religious texts and artwork of ancient cultures worldwide. Proponents argue that recurring motifs like flying objects, supernatural beings descending from the sky, and humans interacting with gods are actually literal descriptions of alien contact. However, a thorough examination of these claims reveals that they rest on flawed assumptions, selective interpretation, and a disregard for the cultural context and symbolic nature of religious iconography.

A prime example is Erich von Däniken's interpretation of the Biblical story of Ezekiel's Wheel. In this narrative from the *Old Testament*, the prophet Ezekiel describes a vision of four living creatures accompanied by mysterious 'wheels within wheels' (Ezekiel 1:16). Von Däniken, in his seminal work *Chariots of the Gods?*, argues that this is a clear account of Ezekiel encountering a spaceship: "The description is not only astonishingly precise, but also extremely technical ... There can be no doubt: the prophet saw a spaceship" [1].

However, this conclusion rests on a literal reading that ignores the symbolic and allegorical nature of Ezekiel's writing. Theologians and religious scholars emphasize that apocalyptic literature, like Ezekiel's visions, is filled with metaphorical imagery and not meant to be taken as a photorealistic depiction of events [2]. The 'wheels within wheels' likely represent the all-seeing power of God, while the four creatures are common motifs representing celestial beings [3]. Extracting these elements from their textual and cultural context and reinterpreting them as descriptions of physical spacecraft is a gross misrepresentation.

Ezekiel's Wheel — Biblestudytools

This tendency to interpret religious visions and encounters with the divine as literal descriptions of alien contact is a recurring issue in ancient astronaut literature. Another frequently cited example is the story of Enoch, a pre-Deluge patriarch who is taken up to heaven and given a tour of the cosmos by angelic beings (*1 Enoch 1-36*). Ancient astronaut proponents argue this is evidence of Enoch being abducted by aliens and shown advanced technological wonders [4].

However, this ignores the symbolic and allegorical nature of apocalyptic literature. The *Book of Enoch* belongs to a genre of Jewish mystical texts that use fantastical imagery to convey spiritual truths, not to record historical events [5]. Enoch's journey to heaven and visions of celestial beings are meant to represent the human desire for divine knowledge and the mysteries of the universe, not a literal extraterrestrial encounter [6].

Similarly, ancient astronaut theorists have long claimed that ancient artwork depicting gods and supernatural beings are actually representations of alien visitors. They point to images like the Palenque astronaut, a Maya bas-relief that seems to show a man seated in a rocket ship, or the Dogū clay figurines of Japan, which have large eyes and peculiar proportions vaguely reminiscent of a stereotypical 'Grey' alien [7].

But again, these interpretations divorce the artwork from its cultural context and ignore the symbolic and stylistic conventions of the societies that created them. The Palenque figure, for example, is almost certainly a depiction of the Maya god K'inich Janaab' Pakal transitioning into the afterlife, not literally ascending in a rocket [8]. The 'rocket exhaust' beneath him is actually the Maya World Tree, a common motif representing the boundaries between the earthly realm and the underworld [9]. The seemingly unusual position and geometry of the figure follows typical Maya artistic conventions for royal portraiture [10].

Lid of the Great Tomb of Pakal — Digitally enhanced — Pixels: Averbakh

As for the Dogū figurines, their striking features and postures are stylized representations of the natural effects of starvation and disease, not aliens [11]. The figures were created during the Late Jōmon period of Japanese prehistory, when the hunter-gatherer Jōmon people faced food shortages and the spread of endemic disease [12]. Exaggerated 'owl-like' eyes, protruding ribs, and asymmetric limbs were likely meant to evoke the wasting effects of malnutrition [13]. Interpreting these as depictions of alien features is not only unsupported, but trivializes the real challenges faced by the Jōmon culture.

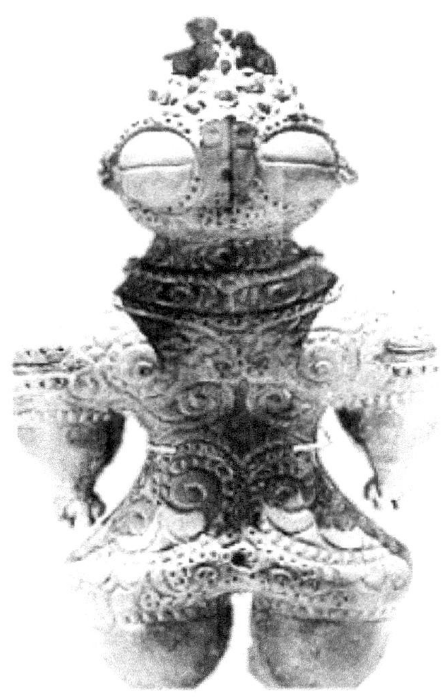

Dogū figurine — Wikipedia

The problem of decontextualization is also evident in claims about prehistoric rock art. Ancient astronaut theorists have argued that petroglyphs and cave paintings depicting figures with strange, humanoid bodies and oversized heads are evidence of early human contact with extraterrestrial beings [14]. They suggest that these images represent alien explorers wearing spacesuits, often pointing to examples like the 'Spaceman' petroglyph of Sego Canyon in Utah or the rock paintings of the Wandjina in Australia [15].

However, these claims ignore the artistic conventions and mythological context of the cultures that created these works. The Sego Canyon figure, with its elongated body and bucket-shaped head, is a classic example of the 'Barrier Canyon Style' of rock art, which features highly stylized, abstract anthropomorphic figures [16]. The unique proportions and geometric features are artistic choices, not literal representations of spacesuit-clad aliens. Similarly, the Wandjina paintings, with their large eyes and haloed heads, depict the creator spirits of the Dreaming, the mythological worldview of Aboriginal

Australian culture [17]. The distinctive features are meant to emphasize the power and otherworldly nature of these beings, not to realistically portray alien physicality [18].

Sego Canyon figure, Utah USA — Wikimedia

Even seemingly direct references to flying objects and aerial battles in ancient texts, like the Hindu epic *Ramayana*, are heavily steeped in allegory and religious symbolism never meant to be taken literally. The *Ramayana* describes Rama, an avatar of the god Vishnu, doing battle with the demon king Ravana and his flying chariot, the Pushpaka Vimana [19]. Ancient astronaut theorists have suggested this is evidence of an actual aerial vehicle and an account of warfare between extraterrestrial factions [20].

However, this claim ignores that the *Ramayana* is an epic poem filled with miraculous and fantastical elements that most Hindu scholars interpret allegorically [21]. The Pushpaka Vimana is not described as a mechanical spacecraft, but a divine chariot pulled by supernatural creatures, similar to other flying chariots used by gods in Hindu mythology [22]. The battle between

Rama and Ravana is a symbolic representation of the triumph of good over evil, not a chronicle of alien warfare [23].

This pattern of divorcing fantastical elements from their allegorical context and reinterpreting them as literal accounts of alien intervention occurs again and again in ancient astronaut literature. Whether it's the Babylonian story of Oannes, the half-fish sage who imparted wisdom to humans [24], or the Australian Aboriginal myth of the Wandjina sky spirits [25], any description of supernatural or non-human entities is taken as evidence of alien contact, regardless of the culture's own mythological framework and symbolic language.

But this approach completely disregards the role of mythology, metaphor, and symbolism in ancient religious traditions. These stories and images were created to convey spiritual truths, moral lessons, and the worldview of the cultures that created them, not to function as objective records of historical events [26]. Stripping away that context and imposing a selective, literalist interpretation to support a predetermined conclusion is not a valid way to study human history or the meaning of ancient texts and artwork.

The idea that religious stories of divine intervention are actually misunderstood accounts of alien contact also fails to explain the striking similarities in mythological motifs across cultures. If these tales were actually based on literal extraterrestrial encounters, we would expect them to reflect the specific physical and technological characteristics of the alien beings involved. Instead, we see common archetypes like sky gods, world trees, divine battles, and supernatural gifts of knowledge occurring in mythologies worldwide [27].

This points to a common psychological and metaphorical foundation for these stories, not a litany of separate alien contacts. Religious scholar Mircea Eliade argued that 'sky god' myths and narratives of divine intervention are expressions of the human yearning for transcendence and connection with the sacred, not historical records of supernatural (or extraterrestrial) events [28]. Similarly, psychologist Carl Jung suggested that the prevalence of certain mythological archetypes across cultures reflects innate structures in the human psyche, not literal encounters with gods or aliens [29].

If we examine religious texts and artwork holistically, within the framework of the cultures that produced them, there is simply no compelling evidence they represent actual alien contact. The recurring motifs of sky beings, flying objects, and human-deity interactions are mythological archetypes found in virtually every culture, likely inspired by universal aspects of the human condition like our desire to understand our place in the cosmos and connect with the divine [30]. They are not secret historical records of extraterrestrial intervention.

The claims that evidence for ancient astronauts can be found in religious texts and artwork rely on a selective, decontextualized interpretation that disregards the symbolic and culturally-specific nature of these works. When examined with a rigorous, academically grounded approach, these supposed depictions of alien contact are invariably revealed to be mythological and allegorical in nature, reflecting the spiritual beliefs and challenges of the cultures that created them, not actual extraterrestrial encounters. This misinterpretation extends beyond individual artifacts to entire mythological systems. The ancient astronaut theory's treatment of these texts and images is a prime example of the 'textualization of evidence' fallacy, where ambiguous or allegorical content is reinterpreted as literal proof for a predetermined conclusion [31]. It is a misguided approach that reveals more about the biases of the theorists than the actual content and meaning of ancient religious works.

Furthermore, the idea that religious stories and artwork are actually misunderstood accounts of alien contact fundamentally disrespects and trivializes the beliefs and worldviews of ancient cultures. It imposes a modern, literalist interpretation that is completely alien to the mindset of the people who created these works. As religious studies scholar Othmar Keel points out, "For ancient man, the gods were not astronauts. They were the forces man experienced in nature and in his own life" [32]. To suggest that the deities and mythologies that were central to these cultures' understanding of the world were actually just misperceived aliens is a form of cultural imperialism, dismissing the validity and sophistication of ancient beliefs.

This is not to say that the question of extraterrestrial life and its potential impact on human history is not a worthwhile one. The scientific search for evidence of alien intelligence, whether in our own solar system or beyond, is a legitimate and exciting field of inquiry [33]. But this search must be grounded in empirical evidence and rigorous methodology, not in the selective reinterpretation of ancient religious texts and artwork.

The fact remains that there is no reliable, firsthand evidence that the gods and supernatural beings described in ancient mythology were actually 'flesh-and-blood' extraterrestrials who interacted with early human civilizations. The stories and depictions of these figures consistently reference their otherworldly, divine nature and are couched in the language of myth and metaphor, not objective historical record-keeping [34]. Cherry-picking elements that superficially resemble modern technology or aliens while ignoring the overall context and meaning of these works is an inherently flawed and pseudoscientific approach.

To further illustrate how religious symbolism can be misinterpreted, let's examine a well-known example from Christian art — the halo, which is known as a nimbus or aureole, being a circular or disc-shaped symbol that is often depicted around the heads of saints, angels, and other holy figures in religious art. This iconographic symbol has been used for centuries to represent the sacred nature, divinity, or enlightenment of the individual it surrounds. The halo serves as a visual cue to distinguish these holy figures from ordinary people and to emphasize their spiritual importance.

The origin of the halo in Christian art can be traced back to ancient civilizations, such as the ancient Egyptians and Greeks, who used similar symbols to represent their gods and divine beings. In early Christian art, the halo was initially used to depict Christ, but it later expanded to include the Virgin Mary, saints, and angels. The halo is often depicted as a golden or luminous circle, symbolizing the divine light that emanates from these holy figures. It can also be seen as a representation of the eternal life and glory that awaits the faithful in heaven. The presence of the halo in religious art serves to inspire devotion, reverence, and a deeper connection to the spiritual realm among believers.

The idea that halos in religious art are connected to ancient alien astronauts is not supported by mainstream historians, archaeologists, or religious scholars.

The use of halos in religious iconography has well-documented origins in ancient civilizations and is rooted in spiritual and symbolic meanings associated with divinity, sanctity, and enlightenment.

The Last Supper, 1304, Giotto di Bondone—Wikipedia

In the end, the ancient astronaut theory's claim that evidence for alien contact can be found in religious texts and artwork is based on a selective, literalist interpretation that disregards the cultural, mythological, and symbolic nature of these works. When examined holistically and with academic rigor, these materials simply do not support the conclusion that ancient humans interacted with extraterrestrial visitors. The similarities in divine/supernatural motifs across cultures are better explained by the common psychological and metaphorical foundations of mythology, not a series of alien contacts.

The desire to find evidence of extraterrestrial influence in our past is an understandable one, given the immense implications that confirmed alien contact would have for our understanding of our place in the universe. But this desire cannot be fulfilled by imposing a predetermined conclusion on ancient religious and artistic works that were never meant to be taken as literal historical records. To do so is to disrespect the beliefs and worldviews of ancient cultures, and to sidestep the rigorous evidential standards that any scientific claim must be subject to.

# CHALLENGING THE ANCIENT ASTRONAUT MYTH

While the question of whether extraterrestrial intelligence exists and has impacted human civilization remains a valid and fascinating one, the answer will not be found in a decontextualized, literalist reading of humanity's mythological heritage. It will be found through the careful, empirical work of scientists and the scholarly study of archaeology and history. The truth about our past and our place in the cosmos, whether we are alone or part of a universe filled with diverse intelligences, deserves to be approached with respect for the factual record, not the misguided reinterpretation of ancient religious texts and artwork. The evidence put forward by ancient astronaut theorists, when subjected to careful academic scrutiny, simply does not stand up. Religious texts and artwork, when viewed in their proper context, provide a fascinating window into the beliefs and worldviews of ancient cultures—but they do not provide proof of alien contact.

## References


[1] von Däniken, E. (1968). *Chariots of the gods? Unsolved mysteries of the past.* Putnam.

[2] Collins, J. J. (Ed.). (2015). *The Oxford handbook of apocalyptic literature.* Oxford University Press.

[3] Greenberg, M. (1983). *Ezekiel 1-20: A new translation with introduction and commentary* (Vol. 22). Yale University Press.

[4] Sitchin, Z. (1976). *The 12th planet.* Stein and Day.

[5] Orlov, A. A. (2005). *The Enoch-Metatron tradition.* Mohr Siebeck.

[6] VanderKam, J. C. (1995). *Enoch: A man for all generations.* University of South Carolina Press.

[7] Hancock, G. (1995). *Fingerprints of the gods: The evidence of Earth's lost civilization.* Crown.

[8] Coe, M. D. (1999). *The Maya* (6th ed.). Thames & Hudson.

[9] Freidel, D., Schele, L., & Parker, J. (1993). *Maya cosmos: Three thousand years on the shaman's path*. William Morrow & Co.

[10] Aldana, G. (2007). *The apotheosis of Janaab' Pakal: Science, history, and religion at Classic Maya Palenque*. University Press of Colorado.

[11] Sakamoto, H. (1998). The Jōmon people and their culture. In K. Omoto & P. G. Asquith (Eds.), *Japanese as a member of the Asian and Pacific populations* (pp. 59-73). International Research Center for Japanese Studies.

[12] Habu, J. (2004). *Ancient Jomon of Japan*. Cambridge University Press.

[13] Nishida, M. (1983). The emergence of food production in Neolithic Japan. *Journal of Anthropological Archaeology*, 2(4), 305-322.

[14] Vallee, J. (1988). *Dimensions: A casebook of alien contact*. Anomalist Books.

[15] Schaafsma, P. (1980). *Indian rock art of the Southwest*. University of New Mexico Press.

[16] Schaafsma, P. (1994). Trance and transformation in the canyons: Shamanism and early rock art on the Colorado Plateau. In S. A. Turpin (Ed.), *Shamanism and rock art in North America* (pp. 45-71). Rock Art Foundation.

[17] Layton, R. (1992). *Australian rock art: A new synthesis*. Cambridge University Press.

[18] Taçon, P. S. C. (1989). From rainbow snakes to 'X-Ray' fish: The nature of the recent rock painting tradition of Western Arnhem Land, Australia. *Canadian Journal of Native Studies*, 9(1), 1-31.

[19] Goldman, R. P., & Goldman, S. J. S. (2007). *The Ramayana of Valmiki: An epic of ancient India, Volume I: Balakanda*. Princeton University Press.

[20] Childress, D. H. (1991). *Vimana aircraft of ancient India & Atlantis*. Adventures Unlimited Press.

[21] Bulcke, C. (1999). *The Ramayana: Its history and character*. Sahitya Akademi.

[22] Hopkins, E. W. (1915). *Epic mythology*. Motilal Banarsidass Publishers.

[23] Thursby, G. R. (2006). The Ramayana. In G. Flood (Ed.), *The Blackwell companion to Hinduism* (pp. 54-69). Blackwell Publishing.

[24] Dalley, S. (1998). *Myths from Mesopotamia: Creation, the Flood, Gilgamesh, and others.* Oxford University Press.

[25] Parker, K. L. (2006). Changing tracks: Predicaments of belonging in Central Australia. *The Asia Pacific Journal of Anthropology*, *7*(3), 205-219.

[26] Eliade, M. (1963). *Myth and reality*. Harper & Row.

[27] Leeming, D. (2010). *Creation myths of the world: An encyclopedia* (2nd ed.). ABC-CLIO.

[28] Eliade, M. (1959). *The sacred and the profane: The nature of religion.* Harcourt, Brace & World.

[29] Jung, C. G., & Segal, R. (1998). *Jung on mythology*. Princeton University Press.

[30] Campbell, J. (1988). *The power of myth*. Doubleday.

[31] Feder, K. L. (2020). *Frauds, myths, and mysteries: Science and pseudoscience in archaeology* (10th ed.). Oxford University Press.

[32] Keel, O. (1997). *The symbolism of the biblical world: Ancient Near Eastern iconography and the book of Psalms.* Eisenbrauns.

[33] Tarter, J. (2001). The search for extraterrestrial intelligence (SETI). *Annual Review of Astronomy and Astrophysics*, *39*(1), 511-548.

[34] Forsyth, N. (1987). *The old enemy: Satan and the combat myth.* Princeton University Press.

# CHAPTER SEVEN
# Ancient mythological roots of the UFO narrative

———

*The UFO phenomenon is not just a modern cultural artifact but a continuation of ancient mythological narratives that have shaped human perception of the skies for millennia. As Carl Jung noted, these sightings reflect deep-seated psychological needs and archetypes that surface in times of collective anxiety*

*Carl Jung, 1958*

*Flying Saucers: A Modern Myth of Things Seen in the Skies*

The UFO phenomenon, a subject of fascination and speculation in modern times, has its roots deeply entrenched in ancient mythology and the collective human psyche. This chapter explores the connection between ancient mythological narratives, religious experiences, and the contemporary belief in extraterrestrial visitations. By examining the works of Carl Jung (1875-1961) and other scholars, we delve into the psychological and archetypal underpinnings of the UFO narrative, comparing and contrasting ancient and modern interpretations.

Carl Jung, the renowned Swiss psychiatrist and psychoanalyst, offered a thought-provoking perspective on the UFO phenomenon in his book *Flying Saucers: A Modern Myth of Things Seen in the Skies* (1958) [1]. Jung argued that UFO sightings were not merely physical events but also manifestations of psychological projections. He proposed that these phenomena were modern expressions of ancient archetypal imagery, originating from the collective unconscious — a shared repository of universal symbols and motifs [1].

Jung drew parallels between the circular shape of UFOs, often described as 'flying saucers' and the mandala — a sacred geometric pattern found in various cultures throughout history. The mandala symbolizes wholeness, unity, and the integration of opposites, representing the self and the cosmos [2]. According to Jung, the emergence of UFO sightings, particularly during times of societal stress and uncertainty, reflected a collective yearning for psychic equilibrium and a sense of order amidst chaos [1].

Interestingly, ancient mythologies across the globe are replete with stories of divine beings descending from the heavens, bearing striking similarities to modern UFO narratives. In Sumerian mythology, the Anunnaki were deities who were believed to have come from the sky to impart knowledge and wisdom to humanity [3]. The ancient Egyptians venerated gods like Ra and Horus, who were associated with the sun and the sky, and were often depicted as traversing the heavens in celestial boats [4].

Similarly, the Vedic texts of ancient India contain detailed accounts of vimanas, flying chariots used by the gods and heroic figures. The *Mahabharata* and the *Ramayana*, two of India's most prominent epic narratives, describe these aerial vehicles in vivid detail, portraying them as technologically advanced and capable of extraordinary feats [5]. These ancient stories not only highlight the imaginative capacity of early civilizations but also underscore a deep-rooted fascination with the idea of celestial beings interacting with humanity.

The Greeks and Romans also had their share of sky-related mythologies. The Greek god Helios was said to ride across the heavens in a golden chariot, while the winged horse Pegasus was believed to soar through the skies [6]. In Norse mythology, the gods were known to travel through the realms in chariots pulled by magical creatures, accompanied by dazzling displays of light and sound [7]. These mythological accounts demonstrate a common thread of celestial travel and divine beings associated with the sky, transcending cultural boundaries.

From a Jungian perspective, these ancient mythological narratives can be seen as expressions of archetypal themes and psychological projections. The idea of powerful, otherworldly beings descending from the heavens to interact with humans may represent a projection of our own desires, fears, and aspirations onto the cosmos. Jung believed that such projections were a way for the human psyche to make sense of the unknown and to bridge the gap between the conscious and the unconscious mind [1].

Moreover, Jung drew comparisons between religious experiences and UFO sightings, noting that both often involve encounters with luminous or numinous objects and beings. The sense of awe, wonder, and reverence that accompanies such experiences is a common thread linking ancient mythologies, religious narratives, and modern UFO accounts [8].

The biblical story of Ezekiel's vision, for instance, bears uncanny resemblances to contemporary descriptions of UFO sightings. Ezekiel's account includes a detailed description of a fiery chariot with wheels within wheels, descending from the sky [9]. This narrative, along with other religious texts like the *Book of Enoch* and the *Apocalypse of Abraham*, contains imagery that closely parallels modern reports of flying saucers and extraterrestrial encounters [10].

Similarly, the Marian apparitions, such as those at Fatima and Lourdes, involve visions of luminous figures and objects in the sky, often accompanied by a profound sense of spiritual significance [11]. These religious experiences, much like UFO sightings, are often interpreted as encounters with the divine or the transcendent, hinting at a deeper reality beyond the mundane world.

While ancient civilizations may have attributed these celestial phenomena to the realm of the gods and the supernatural, modern interpretations often lean towards the extraterrestrial hypothesis. The advancement of science and technology has shaped our understanding of the universe and the possibility of life beyond Earth. In this context, UFOs are frequently seen as evidence of alien visitations, reflecting a shift in our collective worldview.

However, Jung cautioned against a literal interpretation of UFO sightings as physical spacecraft piloted by extraterrestrial beings. Instead, he viewed them as manifestations of the collective unconscious, mirroring the psychological state of humanity at a given time [1]. The Cold War era which saw a surge in UFO reports was marked by heightened anxiety and the looming threat of nuclear annihilation. In this climate of uncertainty, Jung believed that the UFO phenomenon served as a metaphor for the human psyche grappling with the shadow of potential self-destruction [12]. This psychological interpretation of UFOs as reflections of societal anxieties has implications beyond the Cold War era.

Carl Jung wrote a letter in 1957 to editor Gilbert Harrison of *The New Republic* magazine after being invited to contribute an article on flying saucers. This offer was part of a broader strategy to promote Jung's work to a wider audience, leveraging the magazine's platform to reach readers who might be interested in Jung's psychological perspectives. The arrangement was to benefit both Jung, by providing publicity for his book, and *The New Republic*, by featuring an intriguing and topical subject for its readership. The purpose of Jung's reply was to respond to that invitation, to clarify his position on UFOs, and to prevent any misunderstanding about the nature of his work. A copy of that letter is reproduced below.

The UFO narrative has also evolved in tandem with technological advancements. In the late 19th and early 20th centuries, reports of mysterious airships coincided with the development of aviation technology [13]. As space exploration captured the public imagination in the mid-20th century, flying saucers became the dominant shape associated with UFOs [14]. Today, with the increasing sophistication of aerospace engineering and the search for extraterrestrial life, UFO accounts often include descriptions of advanced spacecraft and alien encounters [15].

SEESTRASSE 228

December 12th 1957

Gilbert G. Harrison, Esq.
THE NEW REPUBLIC
1244 19th Street
NW Washington 6, D.C.
==================

Dear Mr. Harrison,
The problem of the Ufos is, as you rightly say, a very fascinating one, but it is as puzzling as it is fascinating; since, in spite of all observations I know of, there is no certainty about their very nature. On the other side there is an overwhelming material pointing to their legendary or mythological aspect. As a matter of fact the psychological aspect is so impressive, that one almost must regret that the Ufos seem to be real after all. I have followed up the literature as much as as possible and it looks to me as if something were seen and even confirmed by radar, but nobody knows exactly what is seen. In consideration of the psychological aspect of the phenomenon I have written a booklet about it, which is soon to appear. It is also in the process of being translated into English. Unfortunately being occupied with other tasks I am unable to meet your proposition. Being rather old, I have to economise my energies.

Very sincerely yours

C.G. Jung.

Retyped letter from Carl Jung about UFOs. Original in poor condition — Flashbak

While Jung's psychological interpretation offers a thought-provoking lens through which to view the UFO phenomenon, it is not without its limitations. Critics argue that an overemphasis on the symbolic and archetypal dimensions may overlook the possibility of genuine physical anomalies [16]. The tendency to reduce UFO sightings to mere psychological projections can potentially dismiss legitimate scientific inquiry into unexplained aerial phenomena. The cultural impact of the UFO narrative and its ancient mythological roots cannot be overlooked. The idea of extraterrestrial visitations has permeated popular culture, inspiring countless books, films, and television shows. It reflects a deep-seated human fascination with the possibility of life beyond our world and a longing for contact with the unknown.

Moreover, the UFO phenomenon has served as a catalyst for scientific investigation and technological innovation. The search for extraterrestrial intelligence (SETI) and the ongoing exploration of the cosmos are testaments to humanity's unquenchable curiosity and the desire to unravel the mysteries of the universe [17]. These endeavors, while grounded in scientific principles, are also fueled by the same sense of wonder and imagination that gave rise to ancient mythologies and religious beliefs.

The ancient mythological roots of the UFO narrative reveal a complex interplay between human psychology, cultural beliefs, and the enduring fascination with the sky and the cosmos. Carl Jung's analysis of UFOs as modern myths highlights the archetypal and symbolic dimensions of these phenomena, suggesting that they are expressions of the collective unconscious rather than literal extraterrestrial visitations.

By comparing and contrasting ancient and modern interpretations of UFO-like experiences, we can gain valuable insights into the ways in which human beings have sought to make sense of the unknown and the transcendent throughout history. While ancient civilizations attributed these experiences to the realm of the divine and the supernatural, modern interpretations often lean towards the extraterrestrial hypothesis, reflecting a shift in our understanding of the universe.

Ultimately, the UFO narrative serves as a mirror, reflecting our deepest hopes, fears, and aspirations as a species. It speaks to our longing for connection, our search for meaning, and our place in the vast cosmos. By exploring the ancient mythological roots of this phenomenon, we can better understand the timeless human quest to comprehend the mysteries that surround us and to find our way in an ever-expanding universe.

As we continue to gaze up at the stars and ponder the possibilities of life beyond our world, it is essential to approach the UFO phenomenon with a critical yet open mind. While some sightings may indeed have prosaic explanations, others may challenge our current understanding and beckon us to expand our horizons. By engaging with this enigmatic subject, we not only seek to unravel the secrets of the skies but also to delve into the depths of the human psyche and the collective mythology that has shaped our species since time immemorial.

In the end, the ancient mythological roots of the UFO narrative remind us that the quest for knowledge and the yearning for transcendence are fundamental aspects of the human condition. As we continue to explore the frontiers of science and the boundaries of our imagination, we carry forward the legacy of our ancestors, who looked to the heavens with wonder and awe, seeking to unlock the mysteries of the cosmos and our place within it.

<u>References</u>

[1] Jung, C. G. (1958). *Flying saucers: A modern myth of things seen in the skies.* Princeton University Press.

[2] Jung, C. G. (1959). *Mandala symbolism.* Princeton University Press.

[3] Black, J., & Green, A. (1992). *Gods, demons and symbols of ancient Mesopotamia: An illustrated dictionary.* University of Texas Press.

[4] Wilkinson, R. H. (2003). *The complete gods and goddesses of ancient Egypt.* Thames & Hudson.

[5] van Buitenen, J. A. B. (1973). *The Mahabharata.* University of Chicago Press.

[6] Hard, R. (2004). *The Routledge handbook of Greek mythology.* Routledge.

[7] Lindow, J. (2002). *Norse mythology: A guide to the gods, heroes, rituals, and beliefs.* Oxford University Press.

[8] Jung, C. G. (1964). *Man and his symbols.* Dell Publishing.

[9] Zondervan. (2011). *The Holy Bible, New International Version.*

[10] Vallee, J. (1969). *Passport to Magonia: From folklore to flying saucers.* H. Regnery Co.

[11] Zimdars-Swartz, S. L. (2014). *Encountering Mary: From La Salette to Medjugorje.* Princeton University Press.

[12] Jung, C. G. (1959). *Aion: Researches into the phenomenology of the self.* Princeton University Press.

[13] Busby, M. (2006). *Solving the 1897 airship mystery.* Pelican Publishing Company.

[14] Ruppelt, E. J. (1956). *The report on unidentified flying objects.* Doubleday.

[15] Hynek, J. A. (1972). *The UFO experience: A scientific inquiry.* Henry Regnery Company.

[16] Sagan, C. (1996). *The demon-haunted world: Science as a candle in the dark.* Random House.

[17] Drake, F. D. (1961). Project Ozma. *Physics Today, 14*(4), 40-46.

# CHAPTER EIGHT
## The enduring appeal of the ancient astronaut theory

*The persistence of the ancient [astronaut] theory reflects a deep-seated psychological need to find extraordinary explanations for human existence and achievements. This phenomenon is rooted in a desire to connect with the cosmos and to attribute our ancestors' accomplishments to external, often extraterrestrial forces, magnifying the mystery and wonder of our past*

*Michael Shermer, 2011.*

*The Believing Brain: From Ghosts and Gods to Politics and Conspiracies — How We Construct Beliefs and Reinforce Them as Truths.*

Despite the extraordinary advances made by modern science in systematically demystifying the universe, the ancient alien theory and its offshoots surrounding archaeological anomalies continue to possess an undeniable power in capturing the popular imagination. What deep-rooted psychological undercurrents enable such unconventional fringe beliefs to persist and even thrive in our contemporary era of rapidly expanding empirical knowledge?

At its core, the enduring allure of ancient astronaut narratives taps into primal human instincts and desires that pre-date recorded history by millennia. We are born explorers: a restless, inquisitive species obsessed with comprehending our cosmic origins and ultimate significance within the grand universal schema. When confronted by the unknown's vast, humbling expanse, conjuring appealing myths and imaginative anthropocentric explanations comes as naturally to the human mind as walking upright.

The earliest creation stories and mythological belief systems emerged as the very first attempts by our ancestors to impose conceptual order and find meaning amidst the whirling, incomprehensible cosmic machinery they witnessed unfolding around them each night in the starry heavens. Those nascent origin myths invariably reflected the psychological projection of humanity's own self-perceived privileged perspective at the time — a perspective that envisioned humanoid deities, supernatural forces, and great hero-beings as the prime movers pulling the cosmic levers of existence.

In many ways, the ancient astronaut theory and the broader fringe historical revisionism it has inspired can be seen as an extension of that age-old overarching human psychology — our species' innate tendency to seek out, contextualize, and imaginatively impose familiar symbolic representations of intelligence, consciousness, and earth-centric importance onto the fabrics of existence even at cosmic scales.

Humans naturally dislike the idea of random chance shaping our world. Ancient astronaut theories offer comfort against this randomness. Some people find it hard to believe that our ancestors could build amazing structures like the Great Pyramid, Göbekli Tepe, or Machu Picchu on their own. Accepting this idea might make humans seem less special or important in the grand scheme of things.

The ancient astronaut theory fills a deep psychological need. It suggests that the beginnings of human civilization were shaped by godlike qualities and knowledge from beyond Earth. This theory claims we were chosen by advanced beings from other worlds who shared their wisdom and technology with us. This idea is more like storytelling than real history, but it appeals to our imagination and desire to feel cosmically significant.

There is also the perpetual longing in the human spirit to not be cosmically alone in the universe driving belief in extraterrestrial observers visiting Earth in prehistory to study our development as a species. The fantasy of advanced alien explorers arriving on Earth in antiquity to covertly witness and perhaps even subtly guide our species' slow evolutionary transition from primitive hunter-gatherers to civilized societies fulfills an innate psychological longing in many to not be so cosmically isolated and alone as an emergent intelligence.

Compounding the psychological inertia of these alternative ancient alien narratives is the predictable pattern of believers eagerly shoehorning and reinterpreting any new archaeological or anthropological discoveries that can potentially reinforce their pre-established belief systems and cosmological frameworks. The human tendency towards confirmation bias and motivated reasoning leads those immersed in fringe revisionist historical theories to readily latch onto any anomalous out-of-place artifact or data point as 'proof' or evidence, no matter how misinformative, that sustains and perpetuates the underlying mythology of ancient alien interventions [2].

The enduring appeal of the ancient astronauts theory is also deeply rooted in its ability to provide simple, all-encompassing explanations for complex historical and archaeological puzzles. In a world where academic disciplines often present nuanced, multifaceted interpretations of historical events and cultural developments, the ancient astronaut theory offers a seductively straightforward narrative that seems to tie everything together [3].

Moreover, the ancient astronaut theory taps into a sense of disillusionment with traditional historical narratives and established academic institutions. For some, it represents a form of counter-cultural thinking that challenges perceived orthodoxies and empowers individuals to question established wisdom [4]. This appeal to anti-establishment sentiments can be particularly potent in times of social and political uncertainty, when trust in institutions may be low.

The role of media in perpetuating and popularizing the ancient astronauts theory cannot be overstated. Television shows, books, and websites dedicated to exploring these ideas have created a self-sustaining ecosystem of content that continually reinforces and expands upon the core concepts of the theory. The visual nature of much of this media, with its dramatic recreations and compelling imagery, can be particularly persuasive, often overshadowing more sober, text-based academic rebuttals [5].

While fundamentally rooted in a foundation of pseudoscience, supposition, and pseudohistory lacking substantive empirical evidence, the ancient astronaut theory and its broader family of mythological narratives nevertheless retain an enduring appeal speaking to deep undercurrents of the human psychological condition. Humanity's ceaseless curiosity to contextualize our cosmic ancestral roots; a powerful distrust and rejection of randomness in the universe; perpetual existential feelings of cosmological isolation and yearning for greater meaning; the tendency to graspingly seek affirming evidence supporting preferred belief systems through confirmation bias; and perhaps above all, the wistful aspirational vision of a cosmos brimming with intelligences standing prepared to join our own embryonic species on an accelerated evolutionary voyage of shared wisdom and consciousness expansion.

As our scientific understanding of the universe grows and solves certain ancient mysteries, new cosmic unknowns keep popping up to take their place. There's always a fresh supply of material for mythmaking, just waiting for creative human imaginations to dive in. Quantum mechanics, theories about multiple universes, the ineffable mystery of consciousness itself — these are all rich new territories where our eternal drive to contextualize existence through stories can find new avenues of expression [6].

In conclusion, while future scholars and thinkers will keep critically examining the motives and psychological underpinnings of the ancient astronaut theory, its persistence reflects our enduring drive to elevate our cosmic status through myth and story even when the evidence says otherwise.

At our core, we struggle with the idea of being an insignificant species in a vast, uncaring universe. The ancient astronaut theory, though not scientifically valid, acts as a modern myth. It helps satisfy our deep human needs for purpose and importance in the cosmos.

<u>References</u>

[1] Kaku, M. (2014). *The future of the mind: The scientific quest to understand, enhance, and empower the mind*. Doubleday.

[2] Shermer, M. (1997). *Why people believe weird things: Pseudoscience, superstition, and other confusions of our time*. Henry Holt and Company.

[3] Sagan, C. (1995). *The demon-haunted world: Science as a candle in the dark.* Random House.

[4] Colavito, J. (2005). *The cult of alien gods: H.P. Lovecraft and extraterrestrial pop culture.* Prometheus Books.

[5] Birchall, C. (2006). *Knowledge goes pop: From conspiracy theory to gossip.* Berg Publishers.

[6] Davies, P. (2007). *Cosmic jackpot: Why our universe is just right for life.* Houghton Mifflin Harcourt.

# EPILOGUE
## In search of ancient wisdom

---

*We live on a hunk of rock and metal that circles a humdrum star that is one of 400 billion other stars that make up the Milky Way Galaxy, which is one of billions of other galaxies which make up a universe which may be one of a very large number, perhaps an infinite number, of other universes. That is a perspective on human life and our culture that is well worth pondering.*[1]

*Carl Sagan, Pale Blue Dot: A Vision of the Human Future in Space—1997.*

Throughout this book, we have explored the enduring fascination with the idea of ancient astronauts — the notion that extraterrestrial beings visited Earth in antiquity and shaped the course of human civilization. We have examined the claims made by proponents of this theory, scrutinized the evidence they present, and considered the cultural, psychological, and scientific context in which these ideas have emerged and persisted.

What we have found is that, while the ancient astronaut theory is a compelling and imaginative one, it ultimately rests on a foundation of selective interpretation, decontextualization, and speculation. The supposed evidence for alien intervention in our past, when subjected to rigorous analysis, invariably proves to be ambiguous, misrepresented, or better explained by terrestrial factors and human ingenuity.

But this conclusion should not be seen as a disappointment or a diminishment of our ancestors' achievements. On the contrary, by recognizing that the remarkable accomplishments of ancient civilizations were the product of human creativity, perseverance, and innovation, we can develop a deeper appreciation for the genius of our forebears and the common threads that unite us across the ages.

---

1. *https://www.sciencealert.com/these-quotes-from-carl-sagan-will-make-you-feel-at-one-with-the-cosmos*

As Carl Sagan so eloquently reminded us, we are the product of a vast evolutionary heritage, the descendants of countless generations of curious, clever, and adventurous ancestors who gradually unlocked the secrets of the world around them [1]. From the first stone tools to the soaring pyramids, from the earliest cave paintings to the intricate mythologies that shaped their understanding of the cosmos, our predecessors laid the foundations for the world we inhabit today.

To suggest that these accomplishments were the result of alien intervention is to do a disservice to the ingenuity and determination of those who came before us. It implies that our ancestors were primitive, helpless, and incapable of great feats without extraterrestrial assistance. This view is not only unsupported by the evidence but is fundamentally at odds with the respect and admiration we should hold for the cultures that have shaped our own.

The achievements of our ancestors are all the more remarkable when we consider the constraints and challenges they faced. Without modern tools, technologies, or scientific understanding, they managed to create architectural marvels, develop sophisticated mathematical and astronomical systems, and craft intricate works of art that continue to inspire us today. These accomplishments speak to the boundless creativity and problem-solving abilities of the human mind.

Consider, for example, the precision and scale of the Great Pyramid of Giza, built over 4,500 years ago. Its construction required not only advanced engineering knowledge but also complex social organization and project management skills. The Maya developed a sophisticated calendar system and made astronomical observations with an accuracy that rivals modern calculations, all without telescopes or computers. The Inca built vast networks of roads and cities in some of the most challenging terrain on Earth, demonstrating exceptional skills in urban planning and agriculture.

These examples, and countless others from cultures around the world, showcase the diverse and ingenious ways in which our ancestors adapted to their environments, developed new technologies, and expanded the boundaries of human knowledge and capability. By attributing these achievements to extraterrestrial intervention, we rob ourselves of the opportunity to learn from and be inspired by the true ingenuity of our forebears.

Moreover, the obsession with ancient astronauts can distract us from the real wonders and mysteries of our past. By focusing on speculative theories about alien visitations, we risk overlooking the fascinating and complex stories of how our ancestors grappled with the challenges of their environments, developed sophisticated systems of knowledge and belief, and laid the groundwork for the scientific and technological advancements we enjoy today.

In the end, the search for ancient astronauts may say more about our own cultural anxieties and aspirations than it does about the realities of our past. In an age of rapid technological change and growing awareness of our place in the cosmos, it is perhaps understandable that we would project our hopes and fears onto the canvas of history, imagining that the answers to our deepest questions lie in the interventions of wise and powerful beings from beyond the stars.

But the truth is likely to be both more mundane and more marvelous. The story of human civilization is one of continuous learning, adaptation, and innovation, driven by the innate curiosity and problem-solving abilities of our species. It is a story of countless individuals and communities working together to build something greater than themselves, passing down knowledge and skills from generation to generation, and slowly but surely expanding the boundaries of what is possible.

This narrative of human achievement and progress is far more empowering and inspiring than any tale of alien intervention. It reminds us that we, as a species, have the capacity to overcome seemingly insurmountable challenges, to create works of breathtaking beauty and complexity, and to continually push the boundaries of our understanding of the world around us.

As we continue to explore the mysteries of our past and the potential for life beyond our planet, let us do so with a spirit of openness, rigor, and respect. Let us celebrate the achievements of our ancestors, not diminish them by attributing their successes to outside intervention. Let us pursue the search for extraterrestrial intelligence with the tools of science and reason, not the speculations of pseudoscience and fantasy.

And let us never lose sight of the profound truth that, as far as we know, we are the only beings in the universe capable of contemplating our own existence, of seeking to understand our place in the grand cosmic scheme. That, in itself, is a remarkable and precious thing, a testament to the power of the human mind and spirit.

By embracing this perspective, we open ourselves to the true wonders of human history and potential. We can draw inspiration from the ingenuity of our ancestors to tackle the challenges of our own time. We can foster a sense of connection with our shared human heritage, recognizing that the same spark of creativity and curiosity that drove our ancestors to build pyramids and chart the stars continues to drive us in our modern quest for knowledge and understanding.

In the words of Sagan, "We are a way for the cosmos to know itself" [2]. Let us embrace that responsibility and continue to reach for the stars, not in the hope of finding ancient astronauts, but in the quest to better understand ourselves and the wondrous universe we call home. In doing so, we honor the legacy of our ancestors and continue the grand human tradition of exploration, innovation, and the relentless pursuit of knowledge.

<u>References</u>

[1] Sagan, C. (1980). *Cosmos*. Random House.

[2] Sagan, C. (Executive Producer). (1980). *Cosmos: A personal voyage* [TV series]. Public Broadcasting Service.

Unsplash—Neom

# VIDEOGRAPHY

## Videography of YouTube clips that align with the notion that ancient humans were capable of remarkable achievements without extraterrestrial assistance.

---

**The Pale Blue Dot**

Carl Sagan, 1994

https://www.youtube.com/watch?v=MnFMrNdj1yY

Carl Sagan's profound reflection on humanity's place in the universe, highlighting the importance of science and critical thinking. This is a short statement of about five minutes.

---

**Chariots of the Gods**

Erich von Däniken, 1970

https://www.youtube.com/watch?v=G-iEXn68Xug

The 1968 book *Chariots of the Gods?* by Swiss author Erich von Däniken, followed by the 1970 documentary of the same name, had an enormous impact on popular culture and sparked a widespread fascination with the idea that ancient civilizations were visited and influenced by extraterrestrial beings. The documentary, featuring narration by von Däniken himself, brought the book's provocative claims to a wider audience, captivating millions with its stunning visuals and tantalizing suggestions of alien intervention in human history. The book and documentary present a highly speculative and selective interpretation of archaeological and historical evidence, often ignoring or misrepresenting the cultural, religious, and technological contexts of the civilizations they discuss. It is this need for a more comprehensive, evidence-based analysis of the ancient astronaut theory that inspired me to write this book: *Challenging the Ancient Astronaut Myth*.

---

## Zecharia Sitchin: Ancient Astronauts Debunked, 2012

https://www.youtube.com/watch?v=j9w-i5oZqaQ

The 2012 video *Ancient Astronauts Debunked* by Chris White is a nearly three-hour, point-by-point critique of the claims made in the popular History Channel series *Ancient Astronauts*, which itself drew heavily from the work of Zecharia Sitchin, a key figure in popularizing the ancient astronaut theory. White's video methodically examines the evidence presented in the TV series, offering alternative explanations grounded in established archaeological, historical, and scientific research. By carefully deconstructing the arguments put forward by ancient astronaut theorists, *Ancient Astronauts Debunked* serves as an important counterpoint to the sensationalized and often pseudoscientific claims that have gained wide circulation in popular media. White's work is a valuable resource for anyone seeking a more skeptical and evidence-based perspective on the ancient astronaut theory, and it highlights the importance of subjecting extraordinary claims to rigorous scrutiny before accepting them as fact.

---

## Scientists Finally Discovered the Truth About the Antikythera Mechanism

https://www.youtube.com/watch?v=LKuLQRzrv2A

This video provides a fascinating overview of the groundbreaking research that has shed new light on this ancient technological marvel. The Antikythera Mechanism, a complex geared device discovered in a shipwreck off the coast of Greece in 1901, has long been a subject of intrigue and mystery for archaeologists and historians. The video effectively summarizes the key findings of a team of international researchers who used cutting-edge imaging technology to decipher the intricate workings of the mechanism. It explains how the device, which dates back to around 150-100 BCE, was used to calculate astronomical positions, predict eclipses, and track the cycles of the ancient Greek luni-solar calendar. The Antikythera Mechanism is an extraordinary example of ancient ingenuity, it does not provide evidence for the ancient astronaut theory or the intervention of extraterrestrial beings in human technological development.

---

### Building the Pyramids of Egypt: A Detailed Step-by-Step Guide

https://www.youtube.com/watch?v=CkyA6ogTGjg

This video explores how the ancient Egyptians constructed the pyramids using available technology and resources. It details the materials and tools used, construction techniques, workforce organization, and engineering insights, emphasizing human ingenuity and effort. The video supports the historical consensus that the pyramids were built by humans rather than extraterrestrial aliens.

---

# AUTHOR

## John Gillam

## Independent Writer On Antiquity

John brings a fresh and enlightening perspective to the topic of ancient civilizations. With a career as a librarian at the prestigious National Library of Australia and extensive experience in the Public Service, he combines meticulous research skills with a deep understanding of human nature and societal structures.

His series of books on *Decoding Antiquity* goes beyond mere historical recounting, instead providing profound insights into what we can learn from our ancient ancestors and the events that surrounded them.

In this book, *Challenging the Ancient Astronaut Myth*, John takes you on a riveting journey through the captivating world of the ancient astronaut theory. He explores the claims, examines the evidence, and unveils the cultural, psychological, and scientific factors that have fueled its enduring appeal. This book is a celebration of human ingenuity, creativity and the unquenchable thirst for knowledge that has propelled our species forward over the millennia.

Contact: John-Gillam@bigpond.com

www.decodingantiquity.weebly.com